RAISING
adam

WHY JESUS DESCENDED INTO HELL

Enthusiasm for *Raising Adam*

From the silence of Holy Saturday, the Ascended One speaks through Gerrit Dawson about the gospel necessity of His descent. *Raising Adam* is a winsome and meaningful exploration of a sacred place that most Christ-followers have not gone. Having confessed the creed for generations, "He descended to the dead" -few understand the relevance and importance of what that actually means. Thankfully Dawson takes us there! Until we understand how far Jesus went to save us, we cannot live into the fullness of gratitude that marks the mature life as one of his disciples. If you descend into the pages of this book, the second Adam will raise you in His life anew.

Rev. Dr. D. Dean Weaver
Moderator of the 37th General Assembly, Evangelical Presbyterian Church
Lead Pastor, Memorial Park Church, Pittsburgh, PA

Diving into the abyss of darkness of Holy Saturday, Dawson engages the difficulty of Jesus' descent into hell. He invites the reader into a much-needed intellectual and spiritual journey into the depths of the inner life of Jesus as He endures the cross and death. This book is a feast spread for 21st century people grappling with the pain and suffering of this world and hungry for hope. It's a "resurrectional" read!

Dr. Susan C. Nash
Church Consultant

Raising Adam explores the purpose of Jesus' absence from all sight and sound between Good Friday and Easter. Guided by the interplay of material from across the Biblical corpus and insight from across the Church's theological traditions, Gerrit Dawson sounds the depths of the Lord Jesus' descent into the extremity of the human condition. This readable exploration, well suited for the thoughtful Christian and pastor, filled my mind with such a portrait of Jesus' humiliation and exaltation that my own soul arose in worship. *Raising Adam* exquisitely demonstrates how good theology leads to nothing less than a devotional encounter with God.

Rev. Dr. Daniel Bush
Pastor, NorthPointe Church
Author of *Undefended: Discovering God When Your Guard Is Down*

Gerrit Dawson is a wonderful example of someone who practices *pastoral theology* — he allows the biblical witness to shape our hearts and minds, and here he calls us to enter into the praise of our humble King. I heartily encourage you to consider his pastoral reflections on these holy mysteries.

Kelly M. Kapic
Professor of Theological Studies, Covenant College
Author of *The God Who Gives: How the Trinity Shapes the Christian Story*

In his eloquently written book *Raising Adam*, Gerrit Dawson beautifully explores how far Jesus went to "destroy the one who has the power of death, that is the devil." Everyone who enters the pages of *Raising Adam* will return from them with a deeply enriched understanding of how fully Jesus descended into our death that he might raise us into his life. It is my great pleasure to recommend it.

Dan Cruver
Director of College Ministries, Heritage Bible Church, Greer, SC
Author of *Reclaiming Adoption*

How far would Jesus go to save us? To go all the way into our desperate human condition, Jesus necessarily "descended into hell." But what does that mean? What actually happened in the tunnel-time between the Cross and the Empty Tomb? *Raising Adam* synthesizes ancient and contemporary thoughts about Christ's descent into a treasure map for readers. Dawson leads us to clarity about how and why Jesus would go to hell and back for sinners like us.

Carmen Fowler LaBerge
Host of *The Reconnect*
Author of *Speak the Truth*

RAISING
adam
WHY JESUS DESCENDED INTO HELL

Gerrit Dawson

Union, Kentucky

The Handsel Press
Edinburgh, Scotland

RAISING

adam

WHY JESUS DESCENDED INTO HELL

A joint Oil Lamp Books LLC, Union, Kentucky
and Handsel Press, Edinburgh, Scotland publication.

Raising Adam: Why Jesus Descended into Hell
Copyright © 2018, Gerrit Dawson

ISBN (print):
978-0-9884916-5-6

ISBN (digital):
978-0-9884916-6-3

Library of Congress Catalog Card Number:
2018954861

∞ The paper used in this book is acid free and lignin free and meets all ANSI requirements for archival quality.

Oil Lamp Books LLC advocates the responsible use of our natural resources. The text paper in this book is Sustainable Forestry Initiative Certified.

FOR KATIE AND JEFF,
HENRY AND CAROLYN

Psalm 139: 7-12
"Even there ..."

Most glorious Lord of life! That, on this day,

Didst make Thy triumph over death and sin;

And, having harrowed hell, didst bring away

Captivity thence captive, us to win:

This joyous day, dear Lord, with joy begin;

And grant that we, for whom thou diddest die,

Being with Thy dear blood clean washed from sin,

May live forever in felicity!

And that thy love we weighing worthily,

May likewise love Thee for the same again;

And for Thy sake, that all like dear didst buy,

With love may one another entertain!

So let us love, dear Love, like as we ought,

--Love is the lesson which the Lord us taught.

Edmund Spenser
Easter, 1595

CONTENTS

INTRODUCING THE DESCENT

How far did Jesus go to save us? Where did he have to journey in order to gather us from the farthest reaches of our separation from his Father? Simply, he went farther than most of us have dared imagine. Jesus entered our mortal frailty and made his way faithfully through this world not only with us, but as one of us. He engaged the dire effects of our sin in his healing work as he undid the ravages of illness, judgment and demonic oppression. But more, Jesus undertook to receive in himself the fatal wounds of our betrayals, the cruel punishment of the cross and the horrifying cry of God-forsakenness. He went to the farthest extreme of human existence. All this he did on our behalf. Jesus came down in order to bring us up. He lived, and died, fully as man in order to reconcile humanity entirely to God. Every time we proclaim the gospel, this is at the heart of the story we tell. One man gave his life for the many. Jesus descended fully into our death in order to raise us fully into his life.

Now, we can tell this news of Christ's saving journey through this world for us by starting with any event in his life and teachings. His every word and gesture leads us to his larger mission. But one neglected episode in particular can take us to the depths of his redeeming work. Though often overlooked, the events of this stage of Jesus' life, death and rising for us can fill us with renewed passion for Christ. They can give us a fresh way to share the ancient story with our culture.

In the center of the gospel sits the silence of Holy Saturday.

Jesus has slipped from the world's view. His body lies sealed away in the tomb. His soul has departed to the realm of the dead.[1] Meanwhile, his disciples hide in fear. Their Lord has died. The revolting sounds of Good Friday keep spilling into the eerie quiet of this dark Sabbath. Jesus concluded his crucifixion with the cry, "It is finished!" (John 19: 30). But his disciples do not yet know that this declaration means anything good but the end, at last, of Jesus' excruciating physical torture. Otherwise, Saturday marks total defeat. For them, it seems the very end of the world. Evil seems to have triumphed while it appears that God, if he exists at all, has abandoned them. On this barren seventh day, those who love Jesus despair.

We'd like to skip this day, passing speedily from bleak Golgotha to bright Easter dawn. But the Father did *not* raise his Son directly from the cross. The Triune God inserted this dramatic pause into the event of our redemption. He insisted that we linger over the realization that Jesus descended fully into a human death. In dying, Jesus' soul separated from his body. The two were not immediately rejoined. Jesus entered the state of *being dead*, this unnatural rending of our embodied existence that is nevertheless, since the Fall, our common lot. Though we never would have written the story this way, in God's providence this day of his absence, his staying dead, formed an essential stage of Christ's journey to save us.

Holy Saturday resides within the earliest expression of our message. Paul passed along what had been taught to him within a decade of Jesus' return to his Father. He writes, "For I delivered to you as of first importance what I also received: that Christ died for our sins in accordance with the Scriptures, that he was buried, that he was raised on the third day in accordance with the Scriptures" (1 Cor. 15: 3-4). We note from this summary that the resurrection was not immediate. It occurred on the *third* day. Until Sunday, Jesus' body remained entombed; his soul remained in a realm beyond our daylight world. The gospel insists on this spacer that keeps us from collapsing the interval between Good Friday and Easter.

Eventually, after centuries of reflection, Christ's church described this silent Sabbath with the creedal affirmation, "He descended into hell." This spare, stark phrase adequately preserves the sad recess before Jesus rose. Yet as gloomy as a descent into hell sounds, for most of the church most of the time, Jesus' descent has been considered a repose for his soul at the least, and, more usually, a day of triumph in the realm below. So the observance of Holy Saturday has been both somber and confidently expectant. On the one hand, the worship practices of the ancient church maintained the solemnity of the day with fasting, the cessation of hymns and the withdrawal of the Eucharist until the Easter vigil. We respect his burial. On the other hand, theological reflection allowed our Easter joy to flow backward upon this Holy Saturday. For after his resurrection, Christ's people discovered that in dying, Jesus was not actually the victim of evil powers. Rather, his death "disarmed the rulers and authorities" (Col. 2: 15). Paradoxically, the shameful cross was the very instrument of his victory. So before rising, Jesus may have been quite busy freeing those long held captive to death as the prelude to resurrection.

In Revelation we hear Jesus say, "I am the first and the last, and the living one. I [became] dead, and behold I am alive forevermore, and I have the keys of Death and Hades" (Rev. 1: 17b-18). On Friday, Christ went down to the house of death, seemingly its captive. But on Sunday he came back with its keys! In between, Jesus took ownership of death. In the 2nd century, Melito of Sardis spoke in words many would echo when he preached in the voice of Christ, "I am the one that destroyed death and triumphed over the enemy and trod down Hades and bound the strong one and carried off mortals to the heights of heaven."[2] Jesus' sojourn in the realm of the dead could thus be understood as a victory march. The first Holy Saturday may have been an interval of hopeless grief for Jesus' followers. But upon later reflection, many considered this a conquering day for Jesus himself. Though his body was in the tomb, his spirit was not defeated but instead plundered hell of its captives.

Interpretative Challenges

So Holy Saturday contains two conflicting moods. This dual sense of sadness and joy has made the clause, "He descended into hell," notoriously difficult to explain. Indeed the episode of Jesus' history which occurred on Holy Saturday remains mysterious. Discussing it is necessarily complex. But noting the sources of this difficulty may help us to understand. There are three main reasons why articulating the meaning of Christ's descent is so challenging.

First, the event occurred beyond the realm of our world. On Holy Saturday, Jesus sojourned among the dead. That "place," or state, is not within the perception of the living. We can't examine what happened to Jesus on this day! It's as if the road on which Jesus traveled entered a tunnel. Reading the gospels, we can see him go in; we can mark where he comes out; but we cannot see what happens inside the tunnel of his being dead. There are no records describing this path he took.[3] We can only make reasonable conjectures based on what the witnesses saw on Friday and Sunday. That gap in revealed knowledge has left wide room for varying, yet faithful and reasonable, interpretations. That we can't fully know exactly how it unfolded complicates every interpretation of the descent and douses us with humility as we approach discussing it.

Second, as we saw above, the descent touches on both Jesus' dying *and* his rising. It connects to his defeat *and* to his victory. We know that Jesus went down a victim and came up a victor. He went down a failure and returned triumphant. He went down in death and rose in everlasting life. In between was his sojourn through death on Holy Saturday. A case can be made that on this Sabbath Jesus rested from his labors, awaiting, with more or less hope, resurrection after his victory on the cross. A case can also be made, as we've seen, that Jesus was highly active on Holy Saturday. In colorful imagery, some church fathers imagined Jesus crashing the gates of hell and releasing the souls that had long awaited a savior. So the meaning of Holy Saturday stretches both backward to the cross and forward to the empty tomb. Our discussions of Jesus' descent, then, are complicated by needing to include both passivity and activity, both failure and triumph, both a sense of futility and expectation in our descriptions. In fact, we cannot understand the descent into hell *only* in terms of defeat or *only* in terms of victory. Without both aspects, we have only part of its meaning. Though complicated to do so, holding the cross and resurrection together, including the different emotions those events evoke in us, is the key for engaging the meaning of Christ's descent on Holy Saturday.

Third, English speakers experience a complication caused by translation and the changing meaning of the word "hell." More modern versions of the Apostles' Creed bring us closer to the original meaning by translating the phrase as "He descended to the dead." The basic meaning is that the soul of Jesus sojourned in the underworld during the time we marked as Holy Saturday. So the Creed was never actually saying that Jesus entered *gehenna*, the future hell of punishment for the wicked that will follow the great Day of Judgment.[4] Still, as we will see, interpretations vary as to whether or how Jesus' experience of this dying and being dead might actually have been *hellish*. Moreover, there is fluidity in the way theologians through the ages have used words we translate as hell. Sometimes they mean merely the realm of departed spirits. Other times they mean a place or state of suffering consequence for sin. Still other times hell refers to demonic powers and their malign intent toward us. Simply correcting the translation of the Creed does not eliminate the crossover meanings in language. The multiple layers of meaning in the concept keep it difficult!

So, amidst these complexities, questions abound about Holy Saturday and the creedal phrase describing what happened to Jesus on that day. Did Jesus descend as a victim *of* death or a victor *over* death? Or both? Was there a struggle in the netherworld? Did Jesus engage the devil, or some form of death personified, in a titanic combat? Or did he remain passive, enduring the diminishment and isolation of a disembodied spirit until the moment the Father raised him? Was this the time when the gospel was preached to those who had died before Jesus came? Did Jesus release the souls who had longed for him in the prison of death? Did Jesus alter the very nature of death by his sojourn in its realm? And what if it were possible that *all* these questions could be answered with a Yes?! That would surely change how we set about teaching this essential episode of Jesus' story.

Underlying Theological Truth

In this book, we will consult the main answers to these questions which the preachers and teachers of the church have made through the centuries. As we go, I believe we will be able to successfully synthesize several differing viewpoints. That's because we will apply a technique seldom used in the consideration of this doctrine. We will explore the descent into hell *as it is set within the whole narrative of Jesus.* The descent makes sense only in context of Jesus' total life and ministry as the Son of God made flesh who came to save us. We will come to understand how Holy Saturday fits as the last in a series of descents made by the incarnate Son of God. When we catch the trajectory of his entire life as a deepening descent into our human condition, the meaning of Christ's sojourn among the dead will open to us. Both sets of emotions, the sorrowful and the joyful, will rise in us through this event. Instead of seeming like a strange interval, the descent will seem like the inevitable next, needed stage of Jesus' journey to recreate us.

The interpretations of the descent into hell do vary across the theological traditions. They can seem hopelessly contradictory. But as we begin our explorations, thankfully we can identify a foundational level of theological meaning to the descent that is common to each major view. At the most basic level, Holy Saturday bears witness to these three realties.

1) A real death

In its essence, the descent into hell means that Jesus truly underwent the full consequence of human sin which is death (Rom. 5: 12). And he did so on our behalf. Christ engaged death in all its spiritual as well as physical horror. He experienced a sense that his Father had forsaken him. He as the Holy One knew the abhorrence of being fully identified with our sin. He went into the void of what Shakespeare called "the undiscovered country" of the dead as a soul sundered from his body. In doing so, Jesus atoned for our sin and opened our way to everlasting life. His victory resounded for all who would believe in him, both before and after his time among us. So Hebrews tells us that Jesus endured "the suffering of death, so that by the grace of God he might taste death for everyone" (Heb. 2: 9). This was so we could be delivered from both the fear and permanence of death (Heb. 2: 15) and be brought as royal sons to the eternal glory (Heb. 2: 10).

2) The last of a series of descents

Moreover, Christ's descent into hell was the last of a series of descents from his incarnation through his ministry and passion. Fully human from his conception, Jesus threaded himself ever more deeply into our humanity as he made his way faithfully and lovingly *as* one of us. Jesus "learned obedience through what he suffered" (Heb. 5: 8), growing in his fidelity even as it was tested by the trials of living in a mortal frame in a fallen world amidst much opposition. He continued in this obedience all the way "to the point of death, even death on a cross" (Phil. 2: 8). Thus by his living and his dying, he fully identified himself with sinners, even, Paul says, becoming sin (2 Cor. 5: 21). It was the cross which dumped Jesus into hell. In this final descent, the Son of God completed his downward journey into the human condition of isolation from God. He reached the farthest extent of his humiliation as the suffering Savior. For Jesus reached the extreme limit of our estrangement from God. It was the last outbound leg of his quest to gather us back home.

3) The turn toward victory

At that nadir of Jesus' final descent, the Father initiated his exaltation as risen and ascended Lord. So, foundationally, the descent also marks the turn from Jesus descending *for* us to his rising *with* us. Paul writes that Jesus "died for us so that . . . we might live together with him" (1 Thess. 5: 10). From beginning to end, God's intention toward us has been expressed in the loving words, "I will walk among you and will be your God, and you shall be my people" (Lev. 26: 12, cf. Rev. 21: 3). He came for us. He would not be without us. Jesus went down, even to the depths, in order to lift us up in renewed communion with the Triune God. He took our death to give us his life. For the Father's banquet table *shall* be full (Luke 14: 23)! Christ's solitary journey into death opened the way by which all who are joined to him by the Spirit through faith might pass from death to everlasting life.[5]

Interpreters vary about the timing and particulars of this descent to the dead, but all agree that these three essential theological meanings belong to this episode. So Jesus' descent into hell is extraordinarily significant for us. For at its core, the descent means: *Jesus descended fully into our death so that he might raise us fully into his life.* That is the heart of what we will be exploring in this book. With this core understanding, the descent can be a lens through which we see more vividly Christ's work of salvation. And, in turn, the life and work of Christ will illuminate this ordinarily obscure event.

Our work will be to trace a series of Jesus' descents in the gospels all the way through to the turning of the story from deepest debasement to highest exaltation. Our hope is to keep vigil with Jesus as his story is told, to keep watch with our minds and hearts. We will accompany him as he goes down so that we might experience how he lifts us up with him.

This means there is much at stake in the event known as the descent into hell. It has to do with just how far the eternal Son of God was willing to go to save us. What happened in Jesus' descent determines the depth of the gospel story we offer. A robust doctrine of Christ's descent, set within the context of his entire life among us, can reach the deep longings in our culture where faith wanes and despair grows. The world aches for a Lover who engages our fragmented loneliness with a pursuit that reaches us even in the most desperate betrayals. We pine for a Redeemer who has exhausted the power of the violence in our hearts by taking it fully, even fatally, into his own heart, returning peace. We crave a companion in suffering who not only empathizes but can give precious worth to our pain. Only a Mediator who descended into the hell of human rebellion against God can conclude our long war with the Father. Only a Christ who willingly received the lethal consequences of our sin can truly take away the burden of them. Only one who has been there, in the hell of our making, can comfort us in our suffering. If Jesus didn't get all the way to the bottom of our predicament, our lost and forsaken condition, then we are left unredeemed at the root. We will be forever lonely, ever tarred with shame, never feeling known, never at peace. But because Jesus entered fully into the deathliness of our human existence, then he can bring us into the eternal life of the Triune God.

Next, to prepare for our journey through the descents of Jesus, I'd like first to introduce the Biblical sources for the descent, and their main theological interpretations.

BIBLICAL AND THEOLOGICAL SOURCES

W hat are you writing about these days?" my friend asked.

"Jesus' descent into hell."

"Oh. So there's like one passage in the Bible about that, right?" He meant the enigmatic passage in 1 Peter 3 which speaks of Jesus preaching to the disobedient spirits of Noah's time.

"Actually," I replied, "You don't need that passage at all. His descent is deeply embedded in the New Testament." He looked at me incredulously. But he was also interested in hearing about the passages. Indeed, far from being based on one obscure and difficult passage, the descent has excellent Biblical grounding. We can follow the Biblical case for the descent by examining five key sets of texts.

First, Jesus predicted his descent to the dead. Immediately following Peter's bold confession that "You are the Christ," Jesus "began to teach them that the Son of Man must suffer many things and be rejected . . . and be killed, and after three days rise again" (Mark 8: 31, cf. Matt. 17: 22-3, Luke 9: 22, John 2: 19). Jesus knew he would not be raised directly from the cross. He anticipated the interval of being dead until Easter. Following his resurrection, Jesus explained to his disciples how his suffering and rising from the dead on the third day were predicted by the Scriptures. His likely reference is Hosea 6: 2, "After two days, he will revive us; on the third day he will raise us up, that we may live before him."

Earlier in his ministry, when asked for a sign proving his identity as the Christ, Jesus offered the prophet Jonah, "For just as Jonah was three days and three nights in the belly of the great fish, so will the Son of Man be three days and nights in the heart of the earth" (Matt. 12: 40). In the Hebrew Scriptures, *Sheol* is the realm of departed spirits.[6] The Greek New Testament uses *Hades* as the equivalent. It was considered to be downward from our life in the world, variously described as under the ground or even under the bottom of the sea. So Jonah described his sinking in the sea, "I went down to the land whose bars closed upon me forever" (Jon. 2: 6). By referring to being in the heart of the earth, Jesus knew that after he was crucified, his body would be entombed and his spirit would be in the underworld across the span of three days from Friday to Sunday. He would be in what is elsewhere called the *pit* (e.g., Ps. 30: 3), cut off from the living, and thus truly dead.

Second, Scripture abundantly declares that Jesus was raised up *from* this state of being dead. His body was raised from the tomb only when his spirit returned from Sheol. Thirty-five times via seven different authors, the New Testament describes the resurrection in terms of Jesus' being raised *ek nekron,* literally "out from dead," that is, away from the company of the dead and the state of death. The phrase implies that Jesus came *from* some place (or state) in order to return to life in the world. Now I believe the ancients knew as well as we do that Sheol is not really a place somewhere literally in our earth, as if we could spelunk down to it. Yet the inspired authors used these spatial metaphors to speak of a spiritual state. Jesus' spirit went *down* to the dead. To describe his return to life, the New Testament uses words about getting up, about rising from being down. So we pile up the directional prepositions: Jesus' spirit came *up-out-from* that underworld in resurrection. We simply must not overlook the obvious. To say Jesus was *raised* necessarily means he had previously descended to the dead. He went down to the place where all departed spirits go, sharing the common human experience of disembodied afterlife.[7]

Third, on the first Pentecost, Peter preached the story of Jesus as he explained the mysterious outpouring of the Spirit. He quoted from the Greek version of Psalm 16, declaring David's words to be about Jesus, "For you will not abandon my soul to Hades, or let your Holy One see corruption" (Acts 2: 27). God promised that death would not defeat his Christ. So Peter declared, "God raised him up, loosing the pangs of death, because it was not possible for him to be held by it" (Acts 2: 24). Even as he proclaimed Jesus' victory, Peter affirmed that Jesus had not been spared the experience of the *pangs*, the severe agony, of the separation of the soul from both the body and the land of the living (Ps. 116: 3). Interestingly, elsewhere the same word is used for the labor pains for a woman (1 Thess. 5: 3) and the birth pains as this age gives way to the new heavens and the new earth (Mark 13: 8). On the Great Sabbath of Holy Saturday, the pangs of death were birth pains, portending Easter Sunday as the first day of the new creation, as Jesus would soon be the firstborn from the dead (Col. 1: 18, Rev. 1: 5).

Fourth, we consider two passages from Paul (who made hearty use of *ek nekron!*). In Romans 10, in a longer discussion on salvation, Paul intriguingly states a question he says we no longer need to ask, "Who will descend into the abyss?" And then he explains why the question would come up: "that is, to bring Christ up from the dead" (Rom. 10: 7). Paul considers the question irrelevant because God has done what no human had the power to do, defeating death by raising Jesus from the dead. What interests us here, however, is Paul's use of the term *abyss* as a place where Jesus was. This was more than a peaceful rest. The abyss was death in the profundity of its distance from any experience of the presence of God, the deep of the deep.[8]

The fact that Paul understood Jesus to have been in the abyss of the underworld lends credence to the traditional interpretation of Ephesians 4: 9. Paul writes that Jesus "had also descended to the lower parts of the earth." Some exegetes interpret this merely to mean that Christ came from heaven to earth in the incarnation.[9]

Yet the very adjective Paul uses for the lower parts of the earth, *katotera*, is the basis for the Greek version of the Apostles' Creed, which affirms that Jesus descended to the underneath, that is, to the netherworld of the dead.[10] Moreover, in Philippians 2, Paul declares that every knee will bow to Jesus who emptied himself unto death but has been exalted to the highest position: every knee "in heaven and on earth and *under the earth*" (Phil. 2: 10). Paul clearly believed in a realm that was spiritual but not heaven, a place through which Jesus journeyed on his way to resurrection.

Fifth, the psalms, and other Old Testament prayers concerning Sheol, open a window onto Jesus' experience after death. David, Jonah, Job and others employed Sheol imagery to express the distress of their dangers and agonies in this present world. Poetically, they imported the dread of the underworld into earthly experience. But in praying such psalms, Jesus knew he would *actually* enter and then return from the very reality of Sheol. While these expressive prayers do not provide us some kind of literal topography of the realm of departed spirits, they do accurately describe the expectation of the state after death. And many offered up for Jesus hope of his return from death (e.g., Ps. 30: 3, 18: 4-6, 49: 15). As Jesus takes up these prayers, new depths of meaning open within them.[11]

The psalms are the prayers Jesus holds in common with us as he, in his manhood, takes his place within the covenant people of God. And they are Christ's distinctive prayer book as he takes up his unique identity as the Son of God sent to save us. As we will see throughout, Jesus quotes from and alludes to the psalms frequently. The Old Testament prayers provided *lyrics* through which Jesus could express to his Father the emotions of his life. Such psalms gave Jesus the words not only to reflect in prayer on situations that had already occurred, but also to enable him to prepare for what lay ahead of him. Their words could carry the spiritual weight of his life, giving him strength for the darkness and hope for a dawn. For example, imagine Psalm 71: 20 in Jesus' passion week prayers, "You who have made me see many troubles and calamities will revive me again; from the depths of the earth you will bring me up again." Or, Psalm 49: 15, "But God will ransom my soul from the power of Sheol, for he will receive me." Also, Psalm 116 would have been sung during the Passover meals in Jesus' day. Consider what these lines might have meant to Jesus just hours before his arrest:

> The snares of death encompassed me;
> The pangs of Sheol laid hold on me;
> I suffered distress and anguish.
> Then I called on the name of the LORD;
> O LORD, I pray, deliver my soul!
> Ps. 116: 3-4

How might these verses have carried him through Gethsemane? This understanding of the psalms means they were written in divine sovereignty not only to express the intent of the human authors, but to create levels of meaning beyond, yet consistent with, their original expression. Even after a millennia of use by God's people, the psalms would have been waiting for use by Jesus the incarnate Son in praying to his Father with and for us during his days on earth. During our vigil with Jesus in his descent, we will invite many of these prayers to illuminate the steps of his journey.

Theological Interpretations of the Descent

So Jesus clearly entered the place, or state, of the dead. But what did he do there? What was the *quality* of that experience like for Jesus? What does it mean for us? Three major streams of interpretation answer those questions.

1) Descending in Triumph

This book actually began in the dark excavations underneath the present Basilica of San Clemente in Rome. I stood before an 8th century painting that is one of the oldest depictions of Jesus' raising Adam. Just two feet from me at eye level, Jesus emerged from an oval of glory. His light seemed to explode into the gloom of Adam's prison. Jesus' left hand held a staff of victory. His determined eyes fixed on our first parent. With his strong right hand, Christ clasped Adam's limp wrist. Adam's other hand extended toward Jesus in open greeting. Jesus had come to rescue him out of this darkness. Below, more was going on. Jesus' foot pressed upon a dark figure prostrate on the ground. I realized he represented the personification of death, evil or both. This was total triumph. Jesus descended into the dead in order to raise all of mankind who would trust him, as symbolized by raising Adam.

That Roman fresco typifies the oldest source of sustained reflection on the descent: Christ goes to the realm of dead as a victor. Hebrews declares that "Through death he might destroy the one who has the power of death, that is, the devil, and deliver all those who through fear of death were subject to lifelong slavery" (Heb. 2: 14-15). In taking Jesus, death literally bit off more than it could chew, swallowing the one who is life in himself.[12] The entry of the Living One (Rev. 1: 18) into the realm of death destroyed it. Having broken its power, Jesus descended to the underworld in order to liberate all the souls of the dead who had been awaiting a savior. This is classically known as the *harrowing of hell*. Jesus plundered death of its spoils and the devil of his captives, setting us free for everlasting life.

The paschal (Easter) prayers in the Eastern Orthodox Church capture the essence of this understanding, as seen in this brief excerpt,

> Thou didst descend into hell, O my Savior, shattering its gates as almighty; resurrecting the dead as Creator, and destroying the sting of death. Thou hast delivered Adam from the curse, O Lover of Man, and we all cry to Thee: O Lord save us![13]

Jesus' descent into hell in these prayers is about the completeness of his triumph. He went down to the root, to the origin, of human nature. All the way to the first man. To dig beneath our sin. To undo the fall. To raise up all that had been lost. Resurrection after such a descent meant healing us from the inside out. This was not only a salvation worked out above us in a heavenly ledger but within our fallen nature as well. As one of us, Jesus the Son of God was lifting us up to his Father in the Holy Spirit.

This view draws on 1 Peter 3: 18-19 in which Jesus, "put to death in the flesh but made alive in the spirit . . . proclaimed to the spirits in prison." If we understand those verses as connected to 1 Peter 4: 6, that "the gospel was preached even to those who are dead," we come close to the traditional idea of the rising Jesus liberating the dead souls who had awaited him. But commentators, especially the ones in my Reformed tradition, remain skeptical of assigning that meaning to the Peter passages.[14] How else could we speak about Christ's descent?

2) Hell on the Cross

By the middle ages, the harrowing of hell interpretation of the descent had been rendered in increasingly fanciful dramas. The spectacle, and speculation, was too much for the Reformer John Calvin.[15] He rejected the harrowing of hell even as he pioneered a theological innovation that continues to have powerful influence among theologians. Calvin understood the "hell" of the creed as more than just the realm of the dead. But he declared that Jesus descended into this hell *while on the cross!* If hell is banishment from the presence of God, Jesus experienced that torturous exile as he cried out, "My God, my God, why have you forsaken me?" (Matt. 27: 46). Jesus' anguished recitation of the first verse of Psalm 22 has come to be known as the moment of *dereliction.* People shunned and spurned him like we would a babbling, weaving derelict on the street. But worse, Jesus experienced abandonment by his Father like a derelict building slated for destruction. The discarding of his body to the lethal cross paled in comparison to the spiritual devastation of his Father's rejection.

Calvin writes,

> No wonder, then, if he is said to have descended into hell, for he suffered the death that God in his wrath had inflicted upon the wicked! . . . he paid a greater and more excellent price in suffering in his soul the terrible torments of a condemned and forsaken man. . . . And surely no more terrible abyss can be conceived than to feel yourself forsaken and estranged by God; and when you call upon him, not to be heard. It is as if God himself had plotted your ruin.[16]

During his crucifixion, Jesus bore the full force of judgment against sin. He underwent the hell of damnation as our substitute and representative. But Jesus suffered not only as a mere man forsaken on the cross. He was the eternal Son of God who had taken up our humanity. This was how one man could suffer on behalf of all. As theologian Douglas Kelly asserts, because of his eternal divinity that was joined to our humanity, those three hours on the cross for Jesus were equivalent to an eternity of punishment.[17]

Building on Calvin, later Reformed theologians could see in Christ's dereliction *on the cross* the remaking of our humanity that the old picture of raising Adam in hell symbolically portrayed. Thomas Torrance writes that the crucified Jesus:

> . . . answered for us to God; even in his terrible descent into our God-forsakenness in which he plumbed the deepest depths of our estrangement and antagonism, he reconstructed and altered the existence of man, by yielding himself in perfect love and trust to the Father.[18]

Jesus' words, "Father, into your hands I commit my spirit" (Luke 23: 46) were spoken into the experiential void of his Father's absence.

Thus, Jesus acted faithfully in our name and on our behalf on the cross. He descended into God-forsakenness, taking the penalty of our sin. Yet he faithfully yielded his spirit to the Father who seemed absent. In this way he raised human nature back into fellowship with God. On the cross, Jesus went into our death in order to raise us up into his life. So whereas our first parents sinned in the paradise of Eden, Jesus obeyed from the hell of Golgotha. In this way he fulfilled his mission to be the last Adam, the remaking of humanity.

3) Solidarity with the Dead

With all the weight of the descent placed on the cross, the Reformed perspective allows the gap in time between cross and resurrection to remain a mystery, declining to fill it in with content that is more speculative than Scripturally sourced. The *Westminster Confession*, for example, states simply that "Christ's humiliation after his death consisted in his being buried, and continuing in the state of the dead, and under the power of death till the third day. . . ."[19] Since the second World War, some theologians have been excavating a deeper meaning of the silence of Holy Saturday. The images from Nazi death camps and nuclear destruction in Japan revealed that increased power and technology leads only to greater capacity for evil. Distended bellies of children from enduring famine, the tidy disposal of the aborted preborn in "health" clinics, and rising suicide rates in a despairing western culture have created a sense that we are in a Holy Saturday world. For many, God seems gone. Hope seems lost. In spite of the wealth we generate, world suffering remains acute. Despair grows. The weak get destroyed with alarming efficiency. We feel in the grip of the day of atheism. In this context, an emphasis has grown on Holy Saturday as a day of defeat and darkness. Its comfort lies in realizing how the Son of God fully identified with our lost and forsaken condition, embracing it even as he overcame it. He received our death and remained in it so that we may know, even in the worst circumstances, we are not abandoned.

Most notably, Hans Urs von Balthasar pioneered the most significant innovation on the descent since Calvin. Balthasar postulates that during what was for us in the world Holy Saturday, while his body lay in the tomb, Jesus entered a "solidarity in nontime with the dead."[20] Nothing was lacking in the atonement Jesus made on the cross. No further active suffering was required. But Jesus' death on the cross meant a real death which has as its natural consequence an entry of the soul into the passive, helpless, free fall state of *being* dead. Jesus, in order to die for us, had to do what experiencing hell on the cross while alive could not do. He had to *be* dead. He had to join those who have passed before us and enter the place to which we are all going; by that, he experienced the full extent of the normal course of the humanity he was redeeming.

Rather than raise Jesus directly from the cross, God the Father made Jesus wait until Easter Sunday to rise. For Balthasar, this means that, at the least, Jesus was dead the way every other person had been dead. He writes, "The fact of being with the unredeemed dead, in the Sheol of the Old Testament, signifies a solidarity in whose absence the condition of standing for sinful man before God would not be complete."[21] Such identification was for Balthasar a necessary part of our redemption. Jesus took the side of sinners even in death, accepting our condemnation fully. Balthasar presses these ideas far past the comfort level of many,[22] and we will consider more of his view in chapter 5. But for now, we can note that Balthasar, at the least, has inspired many recent theologians to take Holy Saturday seriously.[23]

One of those is Joseph Ratzinger, who became Pope Benedict XVI. He was a theological colleague during Balthasar's life. Benedict integrated Balthasar's focus on Holy Saturday into his more mainstream theology. For example, his gifts for clarity and a pastoral touch shine through one of his sermons on Jesus' descent. He understands that Holy Saturday includes Christ's experience of the darkness and solitude of death:

Holy Saturday is ... a unique and unrepeatable interval in the history of humanity and the universe in which God, in Jesus Christ, not only shared our dying but also our remaining in death—the most radical solidarity.

... God, having made himself man, reached the point of entering man's most extreme and absolute solitude, where not a ray of love enters, where total abandonment reigns without any word of comfort: "hell." Jesus Christ, by remaining in death, passed beyond the door of this ultimate solitude to lead us too to cross it with Him. ... Even in the extreme darkness of the most absolute human loneliness, we may hear a voice that calls us and find a hand that takes ours and leads us out. Human beings live because they are loved and can love; and if love penetrated even the realm of death, then life also even reached there. In the hour of supreme solitude we shall never be alone.[24]

Jesus' descent to the realm of the dead during Holy Saturday assures us that the God who has wed himself to our humanity stays with us not only to the end of the age but even through the dark passage of death, even through the deep suffering and sorrow of this present age.

So which is best? Is the descent into hell Friday's God-forsakenness on the cross? The solidarity with the dead in the passive, hopeless suspension of Holy Saturday? The raising of Adam and the harrowing of hell as Christ crashes the gates and subdues the devil in Easter power? Is the descent Jesus' emptying defeat, his rising exaltation, or both? Is it possible that all three of these apparently contradictory themes can be true? After extensively researching the history of this doctrine, Anglican theologian Catherine Laufer reaches a lucid conclusion:

The descensus clause is a paradox: it is part of both Christ's humiliation and his exaltation, the endpoint of his death and the starting point of his resurrection. Between these two points which are paradoxically coterminous, Christ is 'among the dead' as Balthasar puts it. *Thus, the clause is simultaneously about Christ's dying, his being dead and his rising.* . . . By reading the clause in this way, almost as three subclauses, we are able to move towards a reconciliation of the various interpretations.[25]

Each of our three sources for interpretation of the descent can indeed flow together in one understanding! So, the event of Christ's descent into hell touched his dying, his being fully *in* the state of the dead, and his rising *from* the dead in glorious resurrection. To put it another way, the descent was a *bridge* event. It is not only the gap between cross and resurrection, but the vital link between them. It is the "place" where the turn is made from defeat to victory, and Holy Saturday partakes of both. Holy Saturday reveals that Jesus underwent the forsakenness of our sin in himself (as we will explore further in chapter 5). He descended fully into our death, both spiritual and physical. But in doing so, he laid hold of us at the deepest point of our estrangement from God. He descended in order to raise us up with him in resurrection life.

The pictorial rendering of ancient liturgies and icons depicts Jesus clasping the hand of the first man and lifting him out of death, with a multitude following. Whether or not that was a literal event, the theological meaning in this image is that Jesus went farther from his Father than Adam had fallen. He journeyed, as it were, back before the first sin, down to the root of our creation. Then, he raised Adam. Jesus grabbed the man who represents our human nature and condition. Jesus went down, got Adam, and took him with him as he rose. The new, last Adam, redeemed the first Adam (more on this in chapter 6). Jesus completed the recreation of our humanity in the place of the dead, in hell, as rising, he raised us also. This is what it means that Jesus descended fully into our death in order to raise us fully into his life.

Next, to understand this deep meaning of Holy Saturday, we will view the episode of Jesus' descent to the dead as part of the larger journey of the eternal Son's descent to save us. We will follow him, keeping vigil as his incarnation led him through an ever-deepening consecration in a series of descents. Then his final descent to hell will no longer seem fantastic but inevitable, not far-fetched but the expected conclusion to his earlier work. Chapters 2 through 6 thus trace the deepening journey of Christ's descent to save us, all the way to its glorious upward turn in resurrection.

Doxological Treasure

At the end of each chapter, I will invite you to consider Jesus' descent through a different genre of writing: in liturgy, homiletics, poetry and imaginative theology. The first is from 19th century English poet and Biblical commentator Christina Rossetti. Speaking in the voice of Jesus, the poet leads us to consider just how far Jesus descended to save us. She sets his descent to the dead within the entire story of his journey to redeem us. As Rossetti writes, for us Jesus plunged the depth most deep!

"The Love of Christ Which Passeth Knowledge"

I bore with thee long weary days and nights,
Through many pangs of heart, through many tears;
I bore with thee, thy hardness, coldness, slights,
For three and thirty years.

Who else had dared for thee what I have dared?
I plunged the depth most deep from bliss above;
I not My flesh, I not my Spirit spared:
Give thou Me love for love.

For thee I thirsted in the daily drouth.
For thee I trembled in the nightly frost:
Much sweeter thou than honey to My mouth:
Why wilt thou still be lost?

I bore thee on My shoulders and rejoiced:
Men only marked upon My shoulders borne
The branding cross; and shouted hungry-voiced,
Or wagged their heads in scorn.

Thee did nails grave upon My hands, thy name
Did thorns for frontlests stamp between Mine eyes:
I, Holy One, put on gall and shame;
I, God, Priest, Sacrifice.

A thief upon My right hand and My left;
Six hours alone, athirst, in misery:
At length in death one smote My heart and cleft
A hiding place for thee.

Nailed to the racking cross, than bed of down
More dear, whereon to stretch Myself and sleep:
So did I win a kingdom,—share my crown;
A harvest,—come and reap.[26]

Rossetti asks us to consider who else would have dared for us what Christ dared. He "plunged the depth most deep" from his incarnation all the way to his descent into hell. Jesus undertook, in ever deepening stages, to plumb the abyss of death where sin had chained us. He engaged a great journey to gather us home. As we consider this descent, Rossetti's question will lead us to ask our hearts again and again, "Why wilt thou still be lost?" In grateful reply, we will indeed yearn to give him "love for love."

~ 2 ~

LEAPING DOWN INTO OUR LIFE: INCARNATION, BAPTISM AND TEMPTATION

For our sake, Jesus ventured a passage that stretched from the heights above to the depths below. He undertook the mightiest of hero journeys. Leaving the bliss of heaven, he crossed realms in great, seemingly impossible strides. Fifteen centuries ago, a theologian and preacher named Gregory the Great read Song of Solomon 2: 8 and realized he was reading about Jesus: "The voice of my beloved! Behold, he comes, leaping over the mountains, bounding over the hills." Gregory discovered that in his quest to save us, our Redeemer made some extraordinary *leaps*. The first jump down was huge, "From heaven to the womb." Incarnating, becoming what he was not, the eternal Son of God bounded into our very flesh and blood. Then he leaped out into the daylight world "from the womb to the manger" where he began his sinless life of faithful obedience and self-emptying love. In time, Jesus bounded through his ministry, undoing evil and reclaiming people from the darkness. Then, to bear our sins, Christ willingly jumped up, so to speak, upon the cross. This huge leap occurred as the God-man who has "life in himself" (John 5: 26) nevertheless yielded his life for us. In death, he tumbled down to the tomb, but from the tomb he re-bounded back through our world in glorious resurrection. Finally in his ascension, Jesus leaped back to heaven. Yet this too was an extraordinary jump, not a mere return to things as they were, because Jesus took our humanity with him. He took our flesh and blood, now resurrected, into heaven. So he made room for us, conferring a glorious future on all who would be joined to him. To Gregory, Jesus' journey of descending and ascending love truly occurred by leaps and bounds![27]

In our day, William Storey composed a prayer paraphrasing Gregory's imaginative homily. Then, he added a phrase which encapsulates Christ's pilgrimage on our behalf:

> Lord Jesus Christ,
> from the bosom of the Father
> you descended into
> the womb of the Virgin,
> from the womb you visited the cradle,
> from the cradle you came to the cross,
> from the cross to the tomb,
> from the tomb you arose in glory
> and ascended into heaven.
>
> By this great transit of mercy—
>
> you becoming as we are
> and we becoming as you are—
> grant us, O Savior of the world,
> the fullness of our divine adoption
> as sons and daughters of the living God.[28]

Jesus engaged a transit, a passage, through our life in the world to extend God's mercy to us. Storey, a careful scholar, knows that *transitus* is the Latin word used for Passover. Since the time of Augustine, the church has understood Jesus' Passover as his making the redemptive *passage* through the suffering of death into resurrection. By his Passover, Jesus is the sacrificial Lamb whose blood averts God's wrath and takes away our sins.[29] He also is the pioneer and perfecter of our faith (Heb. 12: 2) who crossed death's

Red Sea during his descent to the dead. In so doing, he opened up for us the Promised Land of everlasting life in communion with God. Christ's Passover, his great transit of mercy, is the one event of passion, burial and resurrection that occurred over the three sacred days.[30] This is the heart of Christ's journey to save us.

But both Gregory and Storey lead us to see that this Passover of Christ, his costly passage made to redeem us, may be understood more broadly as well. His passage of mercy includes his entire incarnate life, from conception to ascension. Jesus' descent into hell on Holy Saturday occurred only because Jesus had already, for 33 years, descended into the deathliness of our human condition. He had taken up life as we are (sinning excepted), in a body subject to weariness, hunger and grief. So his descent between cross and resurrection clarifies as we understand it as but one crucial stage of a larger passage. His journey to save us stretches from the heights of heaven through the toil of daily life in a broken world to the depths of death and all the way back again. We seek now to understand the meaning of his final descent by exploring the ever deepening stages of his descent in ministry to us.

The Incarnation

The Patristic writers were fond of saying, "He became what we are, that we might become what he is."[31] Jesus took up our humanity in order that we "may become partakers of the divine nature" (2 Pet. 1: 4). Not of course in a way that makes us God by nature, but in spiritual union with Christ we may share in the Triune relationship of love. We become sons and daughters adopted into the Son of God who became Son of Man. To create the grounds for this communion the Son of God had to engage a precipitous descent into our flesh. God utterly humbled himself. He emptied himself of divine prerogatives and took up our anemic humanity. He made his way among us as fully human, the uncreated One becoming subject to time and gravity, development and decay, the frustration of toil and the slow process of relationship. These famous passages articulate this mystery of Christ's dive into our humanity:

> But when the fullness of time had come, God sent forth his Son, born of a woman, born under the law.
> Gal. 4: 4

> Though he was in the form of God, did not count equality with God a thing to be grasped, but made himself nothing, taking the form of a servant, being born in the likeness of men.
> Phil. 2: 6-7

> Since therefore the children share in flesh and blood, he himself likewise partook of the same things.
> Heb. 2: 14

> And the Word became flesh and dwelt among us.
> John 1: 14

> "The Son of Man came not to be served but to serve" and "to seek and to save the lost."
> Matt. 20: 28 and Luke 19: 10

The Nicene Creed enshrines the heart of these verses in declaring about Jesus, "Who, for us men, and for our salvation, came down from heaven, and was incarnate by the Holy Spirit of the virgin Mary, and was made man."[32] The Son of God descended in order to serve us in love so that we might be lifted up out of sin and death as we are rejoined to him forever.

Baptism at the Jordan

For thirty years Jesus lived quietly, as part of a family, worshiping (Luke 2: 41), studying the Word (Luke 2: 46) and working as a carpenter (Mark 6: 3). All the while he was being prepared for his service as the long-expected Christ, the suffering servant who would save his people. Jesus' public ministry began with a descent. He went down into the waters of the Jordan to be baptized by his cousin John. Jesus, the sinless one, so closely identified with those he came to save that he submitted to a sinner's baptism of repentance.

In a sermon on Christ's baptism, Benedict drew for his audience the line connecting Jesus' journey from his Father's side to the depths of hell:

> That gesture—which marks the beginning of Jesus' public life, takes the same line of the Incarnation, of God's descent from the highest to the abyss of hell. The meaning of this downward movement of God can be summed up in one word: love, which is the name of God.[33]

Christ's descent is a continuum, and all along it runs the love of God who gave his only begotten Son for the world.

It's no accident that John the Baptist conducted his ministry at the Jordan River. This was the river the LORD's people miraculously crossed at flood stage in order, after forty years in the wilderness, finally to enter the Promised Land (Josh. 3: 1-17). The people had to step by faith into the potentially deadly waters before the LORD stopped its flow. If God did not show up, they would have perished. Once crossed, there was no going back. Life would never be the same. Fording the Jordan represented leaving behind the years of futility that had been occasioned by a failure of faith. They embarked at last on receiving and responding to the covenant promises. This crossing, then, symbolically consummated the purpose of Israel's passing through the Red Sea decades before. So the Jordan represented the line between frustration and fulfillment, between wandering and being home. This river had to be entered in faith and crossed by the power of God.

In later Jewish and Christian mystical traditions the Jordan also came to symbolize the dividing line between earth and heaven. This border had to be crossed in faith through dying. Passing through the Jordan meant navigating the polluted waters of the world in faithfulness in order to safely reach the other side. So crossing the Jordan meant a life of spiritually dying to sin and self and living to God. It also meant the final crossing from the exile of this world to home in God's presence. Baptism in the Jordan anticipates Jesus' Passover journey through a sinless life to the cross and into resurrection. The book of Hebrews places Psalm 40 on the lips of Jesus. As he made his way down the Jordan's banks, we can well imagine that this was a time for him to pray, "Behold I have come to do your will, O God, as it is written of me in the scroll of the book" (Heb. 10: 7).

Conquering Chaos and Evil

Geographically, we can see why such symbolism grew around this river. Three springs to the north create the tributaries that become the Jordan. One is near the ancient city of Caesarea-Philippi. There a spring flowed from the mouth of a cave near the bottom of a huge rock cliff. This stony hill was known as the Rock of the Gods. Numerous pagan temples have been excavated there. One marked the worship of Baal, the perennial tempter of Israel to idolatry. It was said that Baal could come and go from the underworld through the waters of this cave. When the Greeks came, they marked this cave with a shrine to the god Pan. Nearby, sexual rites of dedication, including bestiality, would take place.[34]

By Jesus' day, there was also a temple to Caesar, hailing the emperor as a god. So these headwaters flowed from a place triply identified with humanity's rebellious idolatry.

The cave at the headwaters itself came to be called by the Greeks the "Gates of Hades." Waters came forth from this dark shaft of seemingly endless descent. To the imagination, it looked like the very opening to the realm of the dead. Strikingly, Jesus was in Caesarea-Philippi when he declared that the Gates of Hades could not stand against his church (Matt. 16: 18). He meant for his gospel to advance against even the most hellish places. The Jordan River ends at the geographically lowest place on earth, the Dead Sea, so salty that nothing can live in its waters. The very topography of the Jordan lends itself to symbolism as life coming out of the depths and flowing to death, as a border between life and death, and as a dividing line between this world and the next.[35]

The waters were associated with death. So entering the Jordan for baptism, then, meant symbolically dying to one's old life of sin and rising to a new life committed to righteousness. In this way, the baptism of Jesus anticipated his death on the cross, his descent to the dead and his resurrection from the tomb. The early church saw links between Jesus' descent into the Jordan and his descent into hell. Baptist patristic scholar Everett Ferguson discovered numerous examples from the early church of how Jesus' "baptism was interpreted as a struggle with Satan in which Jesus descended into a watery grave, an image of Satan's underworld abode, and came up victorious, in anticipation of his later descent into Hades and victorious emergence from death."[36]

Benedict also weighs the meaning in this ancient idea that Christ's baptism symbolized and anticipated a conquering combat with the evil one. He writes,

> . . . He goes down in the role of one whose suffering-with-others is a transforming suffering that turns the underworld around, knocking down and flinging open

the gates of the abyss. His Baptism is a descent into the house of the evil one, combat with the "strong man" (Luke 11: 22) who holds men captive (and the truth is we are all very much captive to powers that anonymously manipulate us!). Throughout all its history the world is powerless to defeat the "strong man;" he is overcome and bound by one yet stronger, who, because of his equality with God, can take upon himself all the sin of the world and then suffers it through to the end— omitting nothing on the downward path into identity with the fallen.[37]

This first public action of Jesus, then, previews the whole course of his victorious struggle with evil and his transformation of the cosmos from the inside out by his triumphant dying and rising. It shows his descending into our death in order to raise us into his everlasting life.

From Confirmation to Temptation

Immediately after this event, Jesus went out to the wilderness to have that newly consecrated will tested to the extreme. He had come to do his Father's will. Now that intent would be challenged by the powerful, nearly overwhelming currents of temptation to self-assertion. Matthew recounts, with a mastery of understatement, "Then Jesus was led up by the Spirit into the wilderness to be tempted by the devil. And after fasting forty days and forty nights, he was hungry" (Matt. 4: 1-2). Jesus denied himself food to the point of extreme weakness, risking his body's ability to come back to health. He went out to a place without human society or any built habitation. The sands ran away in every direction under the heat of an unrelenting sun. The conditions warranted the unraveling of coherence, the swirling of once clear intentions, and the blurring of the line between reality and illusion. In this sense, Jesus descended beyond any reasonable and customary tests of keeping God's will when tempted with doing otherwise. He was vulnerable to falling.

We cannot help but draw a sharp contrast between the conditions of temptation between the first Adam and the last Adam. Our first parents lived in a state of plenty, with fruit available at all times all around them. They walked with the LORD God and spoke to him face to face. They had only one law to keep. The Garden was bordered by rivers to keep it lush and provide a sense of protection. They lived in paradise, and fell into disobedience even when the environment for obedience was ideal. To undo their disaster amidst the best circumstances, Jesus had to encounter and defeat the evil one in the harshest conditions.

So the tempter came and said to him, "If you are the Son of God. . . ." (Matt. 4: 3). Each of the three temptations begins with a challenge to the voice of the Father spoken at Jesus' baptism. We hear the echo of the serpent's words in the Garden of Eden, "Did God actually say. . . ." (Gen. 3: 1). At the heart of every temptation is the enticement to think one knows better than God, to follow the desire to be other than what God declares us to be, to seize control under the illusion that there is a destiny better than God's will. In all three temptations, Jesus responded not by relying on his immediate impulses, or even the information coming from his senses. He framed every answer with the words, "It is written. . . ." In this way he consecrated his human will against every shortcut to his Father's vision.

Hebrews assures us, "Therefore he had to be made like his brothers in every respect, so that he might become a merciful and faithful high priest in the service of God, to make propitiation for the sins of the people. For because he himself has suffered when tempted, he is able to help those who are being tempted" (Heb. 2: 17-18). Jesus not only came down to experience our mortal frailty, but also endured strong temptation to sin. He descended into the fierce urging to seize something that appears good or needed in the moment against the wisdom of God's Word and enduring will for us. So acute was Jesus' sensitivity to sin that he suffered far more than we do in his resistance to all evil. With each temptation, Jesus declined using the power at his disposal. He had emptied himself to be like us and would not "cheat" by supernaturally getting out of his hunger or garnering the power of the world. As he would have to do in Gethsemane and on the cross, Jesus relied on the Word of God in sheer faith. And from there temptation yielded to joy. Jesus could pray on the other side of temptation with Psalm 73, "God is the strength of my heart and my portion forever." Thus he was ready to return to enter even more deeply into the darkness of our life in captivity to sin and its consequences.

Doxological Treasure

In one of the greatest baptismal sermons of all time, the fourth century theologian, Gregory of Nazianzen, preached on the significance of Christ's baptism as a type of his descending and rising:

Jesus rises from the waters; the world rises with him. The heavens like Paradise with its flaming sword, closed by Adam for himself and his descendants, are rent open. The Spirit comes to him as to an equal, bearing witness to his Godhead. A voice bears witness to him from heaven, his place of origin. The Spirit descends in bodily form like the dove that so long ago announced the ending of the flood and so gives honor to the body that is one with God.

Today let us do honor to Christ's baptism and celebrate this feast in holiness. Be cleansed entirely and continue to be cleansed. Nothing gives such pleasure to God as the conversion and salvation of men, for whom his every word and every revelation exist. He wants you to become a living force for all mankind, lights shining in the world. You are to be radiant lights as you stand beside Christ, the great light, bathed in the glory of him who is the light of heaven. You are to enjoy more and more the pure and dazzling light of the Trinity, as now you have received - though not in its fullness - a ray of its splendor, proceeding from the one God, in Christ Jesus our Lord, to whom be glory and power for ever and ever. Amen.[38]

Jesus went down into the filthy waters of the Jordan, the unredeemed creation, as the sinless one in our sinful world and frail flesh. He consecrated himself to the task of our renewal. He did what the old Adam failed to do. He conquered temptation. He obeyed. He descended into the waters of death which symbolize the dominion of the evil one. But, victorious by his consecration, he rose from the river that now represents the waters of new birth. Jesus came up set aside as the new man in our old world, the new head of the human race. He is the one who symbolically takes all creation with him in this descent and ascent. Thus, his baptism is the type of the whole story of Jesus' journey of salvation. It is both his acceptance and preview of his passion. This is the meaning of Gregory's declaration that as Jesus rises from the waters, the whole world rises with him. His baptism is a preview, an earnest, of how in him the new creation will rise from the old. Jesus in his emergence from the Jordan, in his ministry amidst evil and brokenness, and in his rising from the hell of the cross and the realm of the dead, led forth proleptically all the old creation that is being restored.

~ 3 ~

DOWN TO THE CAPTIVES: DESCENDING INTO MINISTRY

The great transit of mercy which Jesus engaged for us ran along two tracks. Jesus ran the course in which he received the consequences of sin: of being born in a body that dies, subject to weakness and temptation. Along the way he endured and engaged the deathliness of our living. He followed this path all the way to entering condemnation and forsakenness. Jesus also ran the course of human obedience that leads to life. Within our weak frame, he lived faithfulness as no human had before. So Jesus brought the two tracks together. He made the passage of a faithful human life through death and hell then back into life. We become passengers in his journey when we are joined to him by faith through the uniting work of his Holy Spirit. We can become participants in his everlasting life and in his mission to gather still more into his story.

Empowered by the Spirit, Jesus would descend further into the hellish conditions of our existence. He would behold, touch, and engage humanity in the worst bondage and in the fiercest opposition to God. In his ministry, Jesus dove down to encounter those who have been broken by humanity's breaking of the Father's will. In those murky cold waters, Jesus laid hold of men and women in bondage to illness, possession, dysfunction and death. He brings them up into the warm light of his grace. Their earthly healing becomes the foretaste of their participation in a restored and glorified humanity. For as they respond in faith they become joined to the new Adam, the head of a remade humanity. We will keep watch with Jesus now as he encounters three historic enemies of humankind: sin, death and the devil.

Descending to the Circle of Shame

In John 8: 1-11, we read that early one morning Jesus went to the temple in Jerusalem.[39] He was in the great outer court, the very center of life in that city. There he sat and taught, and throngs of people came out to him. Suddenly he was interrupted by a disturbance passing through the crowd. The religious leaders had also gotten up early. So early that they caught a woman in bed with a man not her husband. They dragged her from the house and dumped her before Jesus. Their faces were flush with anger and their eyes flashed danger. "Teacher, this woman was caught in the act. The law says we should stone her. What do you say?" Very quickly, the circle of supposed learners of the Word became a circle of condemnation. And they placed the woman within their sphere of shame. The self-righteous were twitching with anticipation. If this worked, they'd get a good stoning out of it and Jesus' famous compassion would be tarnished forever. Otherwise, if he failed to support the law, Jesus would be a law-breaker and they could arrest him.

Jesus, however, had the strength to absorb the urgent energy of the stoning mob. He slowed them down. Jesus the righteous one stood *with* the sinful woman in the circle of shame. This was the working out of his baptism. Jesus had received a sinner's baptism, not because of his sin, but because he came to stand with us in our sin. So now he lived it out, identifying with the sinner. He stood on her (and therefore our!) side of the line. Then he called for a volunteer to pitch the first rock! But there was a qualification. "The one of you without sin, let him cast the first stone." His words hung in the air with power. The one who would declare before Jesus and his peers that he had *no* sin could let it fly. One by one, eldest to youngest, they dropped their stones and left.

Jesus the sinless one was uniquely in a position justly to punish sin. But instead he stayed with her. "Woman, where are they? Has no one condemned you?" I imagine she answered quietly, with rising relief turning into amazement, "No one, Lord." Then Jesus said the most wonderful words, "Neither do I condemn you! Go, and from now on, sin no more." *Neither do I condemn you.* He knew what she did. He knows what each of us does, what we think, what we feel. He knows that the Accuser hunts us down with his tirades. "You are not good enough. You have done wrong and will again. You are not lovable. You are not forgivable. If they only knew, you'd be out. You are *not* worthy." But Jesus silences the accusations. He knows all. He knows we come by our sins honestly, often seeking relief through wrong means. He knows all the circumstances that lead to the things we do. He knows the depths of each depraved heart that give rise to how we respond to situations and temptations. And he stands in the circle of shame with us, willing to take the stones we have earned. "Neither do I condemn you. Not because you didn't sin. You did. But I am the only judge. And I forgive. For I paid, in full, for your sin. Go and sin no more." So Paul would tell us in Romans 8: 1, "There is now no condemnation for those who are in Christ Jesus." Jesus, Immanuel, God with Us, descended from the seat of judgment to abide within the circle of shame with the woman and declare his victory over her sin.

Descending to All Our Dying

In Luke 7: 11-17, we read that Jesus and his disciples were coming to a town called Nain. Jesus had accumulated a great crowd of followers, meaning a veritable parade of people was approaching the city gate. But just then another crowd was coming *out* of the gate. It was a funeral procession. They were carrying a body out to be buried in a tomb. Two large groups of people were heading for collision. Even in our jaded culture, we would expect the funeral to take precedence. Imagine what would happen if someone with a great crowd behind him stepped out in front of the hearse and stopped the procession. People would be outraged for the impertinence. But Jesus did not turn aside.

As the two crowds drew near each other, Jesus noticed the situation. He saw that the young man on the bier was being mourned by one woman in particular. She was a widow who had lost her only son. As he beheld her grief and the uncertainty in her future with no one to care for her, Jesus was deeply moved. Compassion filled him.[40] Upon seeing her situation, Jesus' heart went out to this woman. So he stopped the funeral. He spoke to the startled woman. "Don't cry." Then he did the unthinkable. He touched the bier. That in itself would have made him unclean, and would have been seen as incredibly rude. But before anyone could remove him, Jesus spoke to the dead man, "Young man, I say to you, arise!" And the dead man sat up and began to speak. Jesus directed him to his mother whose wailing grief had turned to the laughter of joy.

The only begotten Son of the Father encountered the funeral procession of an only son of his mother, and she a widow. The Lord of life encountered the reality of all our dying. Sin brought death into the world. Jesus came to atone for sin and restore everlasting life. Seeing the woman's loss, Jesus was moved deeply in his heart. He outrageously stopped the funeral. He spoke to the widow: do not weep. Jesus engaged the clash between the steady procession of death and his eternal life, between his holiness and the uncleanness of the dead body, between his joy and our despair. He came all the way down to the places where we carry out our sons and daughters to the grave. And he stopped the dreadful flow. He turned death back into life. This moment was a foretaste of the resurrection he will bring to all who look to him. All our dying has not ended yet. But this miracle was a sign of what is to come. Jesus who would pass through death to resurrection will call a halt to all this death.

He will create glorious reunions. He gives us hope in the midst of sorrow.

Down to the Chaos of our Madness

In Mark 5: 1-20 we meet the man known as Legion. He was so afflicted by evil spirits that he could not live in normal human company. He lived out among the tombs. The townspeople tried to chain him up, but he would break his chains and go on rampage. Legion had long since shed his clothes. He howled day and night. He found stones and gashed himself. This was the kind of man most would avoid at all costs.

Jesus crossed the sea from Israel to the pagan land of Gerasene. This perhaps was the ugliest, most forsaken place to which Jesus went in his sojourn among us. He came down and went out to a place of tombs across the sea. He came ashore very near the city of the dead that Legion haunted. This was a sign that the kingdom of God was breaking beyond national boundaries to spread to the whole world. And it was a sign that there was no place Jesus would refuse to go in order to save the lost. He went to the regions of madness. He went to the demon-infested lands. He went to the place of howling pain. He went to those so tormented they cut themselves and bashed themselves and made themselves throw up good food. Jesus did not despise even Legion. He did not turn even from this seemingly unreachable wretch.

As with the raising of the widow's son, this action was a sign pointing to the future hope of the kingdom of God. By the end of the story, the man once possessed was sitting clothed and in his right mind at the feet of Jesus. He was restored. Though few have such dramatic affliction, multitudes will testify to this peace-creating power in the presence of Jesus. They tell us of the order Christ brings out of chaos. They tell us of the hope he brings to despair. They tell us how he turns ashes into beauty. It doesn't often happen as instantly as it did with Legion. But over time, with the care of God's people and the steady participation in the Word of God and the life-giving power of his Holy Supper, we become clothed, in our right minds, peaceful at the feet of Jesus.

The man once known as Legion wanted to follow Jesus back to Israel. But instead, Jesus sent him to his own people. "Go home to your friends and tell them how much the Lord has done for you, and how he has had mercy on you" (Mark 5: 19). The irony is not lost here. Legion had no friends during his demoniac state. He was as lonely as a man can be. But the one who descended even to the madness of his possession recreated him for relationship. So he began to proclaim in Greek lands "how much *Jesus* had done for him" (Mark 5: 20).

Raising Adam: The Demonized Boy

Mark records an episode in Jesus' ministry that is paradigmatic of Christ's whole transit of mercy toward us (Mark 9: 14-29). The setting is Jesus' return from being transfigured on the mountain. On the heights, Jesus' heavenly glory had shone through his humanity. Luke records that he spoke there with Elijah and Moses about his impending exodus (Luke 9: 31). This event, then, was meant to strengthen Jesus as his journey turned toward his Passover through death back to his Father. In fact, a heavenly voice confirmed what had been said at Jesus' baptism, "This is my beloved Son" (Mark 9: 7). So on the mountain of transfiguration, the whole journey has been reiterated in concentrated form. The beloved Son for a moment partook of his origin in heaven, even as he prepared to descend back to the world and sojourn through the final battle.

As Jesus went down, he encountered a commotion. His disciples had been unable to heal a boy whose demonic affliction was particularly disturbing. His symptoms included being chronically mute while experiencing frequent seizures. The disciples' messy attempt at exorcism had drawn a crowd. Jesus surveyed the scene and lamented, "O faithless generation, how long am I to be with you?" When the boy was brought, the presence of Jesus provoked a violent convulsion. The evil spirit threw the boy to the ground, where he rolled about, foaming at the mouth. The father entreated Jesus, "If you can do anything, have compassion on us and help us." Jesus replied, almost sarcastically "If you can!" Then he added, "All things are possible for one who believes." The father cried out desperately, "I believe; help my unbelief!" As expected, Jesus cast out the spirit. But the effect on the boy was surprising. Though the demon left, it took a parting shot, convulsing the boy so terribly that he fell down "like a corpse (*nekros*)." Most of the crowd declared, "He is dead." Jesus, however, took the boy "by the hand and lifted him up, and he arose."

We hear echoes of our thesis. Jesus descended fully into our death. He came down from the mountain of glory into the chaos of demonic oppression in a faithless world. Jesus did not turn away from the ugly scene. Nor was he dismayed when his presence appeared to make things worse. He did not hesitate to risk the mockery of the cynical crowd as he took a dead child by the hand and raised him. Mark, of course, placed the same word on the angel's lips in declaring Christ's resurrection: He has risen! (Mark 16: 6). Jesus raised the boy by the power of his own indestructible life (Heb. 7: 16).

How can we not also see in this account a source of the image of Jesus' raising Adam in the realm of the dead? Adam, whose faithlessness plunged the world into darkness, languished in the realm of the dead, the epitome of human failure. The accuser would chatter ever after that this is the fate of men which could never be undone. But all things were possible to Christ who lived perfect faith in his Father. In his ministry, he went down among us, in all our lost and forsaken circumstances in order to lift us up. In many circumstances over these three years, Jesus took the limp wrist of dead humanity and raised us back into life.

Doxological Treasure

In his ministry as well as his incarnation, Jesus grasped our humanity, our existence in time and flesh, and made it his own. In his book *Miracles*, C.S. Lewis describes "this huge descent and re-ascension in which God dredged the salt and oozy bottom of Creation."[41] With two striking metaphors, that of a strong man and a pearl diver:

> In the Christian story, God descends to re-ascend. He comes down; down from the heights of absolute being into time and space, down into humanity; down further still . . . down to the very roots and seabed of the Nature He has created. But He goes down to come up again and bring the whole ruined world up with Him. One has the picture of a strong man stooping lower and lower to get himself underneath some great complicated burned. He must stoop in order to lift, he must almost disappear under the load before he incredibly straightens his back and marches off with the whole mass swaying on his shoulders.
>
> Or one may think of a diver, first reducing himself to nakedness, then glancing in mid-air, then gone with a splash, vanished, rushing down through green and warm water into black and cold water, down the increasing pressure into the deathlike region of ooze and slime and old decay; then up again, back to colour and light, his lungs almost bursting, til suddenly he breaks the surface again, holding in his hand the dripping, precious thing he went down to recover.[42]

Jesus is a pearl fisher. In his descent to us, he dove deep in order to retrieve something of inestimable value to his Father. Something that has been lost, something that actually *got itself* lost. But also something that, in the mystery of God's providence is being made more beautiful down in these depths, at such a price to recreate and retrieve, than it had been originally. We, Christ's bride, his church, even in our fallen humanity are together that pearl for which he stakes his life to gather. Each stage of Christ's descent in ministry was another, deeper dive of the pearl fisher. On each plunge into the cold darkness beneath Jesus gathered up further dimensions of what was lost. But after the days of his ministry, Jesus would have to dive deeper still into our lost and forsaken condition to retrieve us.

STRAINING THE ETERNAL BONDS: GETHSEMANE AND GOOD FRIDAY

The pearl of great price to the Triune God is the human heart freely willing obedience to the Father, for in such faithful love we participate as image bearers of God. We enter the glory of God's eternal life as the One who has his very being in the love of the Father, Son and Holy Spirit. Jesus dove deep into our humanity to recover that fidelity and so restore us to our proper place in God. But our heart of obedience could not be generated in ourselves. We would have to be *re*-generated. A faithful human spirit would have to be established anew in Jesus. To do so, Jesus would have to enact a lovingly obedient will in the midst of the most extreme pressure to turn aside. His engagement with the evil one in his dire trials in the wilderness prepared Jesus for the hours of his passion. But by comparison, these temptations were only a foretaste of the soul's agony he would encounter in Gethsemane. Jesus would have to willingly descend into the exact opposite of his heart's desire to be in communion with his Father. His love for us in the eternal Triune plan would require him to enter the hell of God-forsakenness.

During what we have come to call Holy Week, opposition to Jesus reached its inevitable conclusion. Eventually, the religious leaders made a definite decision to have Jesus arrested and brought to Roman trial. At the same time, Jesus' own disciple Judas became ready to hand over his master. People and powers moved against

Jesus. But the reality was that Jesus orchestrated events so that his passion would occur at the feast of Passover. He would be the Paschal lamb. He would lead his people through the sea of death to the Promised Land of communion and life.

That last night, Jesus and his disciples shared the sacred feast of God's people known as the Passover, or Pascha. As they do to this day, the Jews celebrated how the LORD I AM had led his people out of slavery with mighty acts of redemption. They remembered that when the angel of death was sent to slay the firstborn of Egypt, the angel passed over those houses on which the blood of a lamb had been placed on the door. Hence, the name of the feast became "Passover." God had passed over the homes of his people during the plague. Then the LORD led his people to pass over the Red Sea as if it were dry land. The Exodus itself was a kind of Passover, as was the crossing of the Jordan into the Promised Land forty years later. Centuries later, Israel's return to the land after seventy years of exile in Babylon was also considered an exodus and a Passover. And the people waited for the final Passover, when God himself would come and lead his people to the freedom of his kingdom on earth.

A fourth century homily describes how Jesus symbolically gave himself in the supper before the powers enacted their will against him, showing that he was in control of events:

> A feast he prepared for his Bride, to allay her hunger. Our Lord slew his own body, and (only) then did mortals slay it. He pressed it out into the cup of salvation and (only) then did the People also press it out on the cross. . . . The Lamb ate the lamb, the Pascha [Passover] consumed the Pascha. He brought his Father's institution to an end and began his own; he concluded the Law and inaugurated the new covenant of reconciliation.[43]

Jesus arranged to be crucified to die just at the time the Passover lambs were being slaughtered. He was buried just before a day of Sabbath rest so that he could rise as a new creation on the first day of the week. For anyone who knows how difficult it can be just to transfer an automobile title in one attempt, this influence of the Roman and Jewish bureaucracies to suit his purposes is nothing short of divine intervention. Only a brilliant, savvy leader could have timed events with such an eternal perspective.

Entering Sorrow

That's the sovereign side of Christ's descent into betrayal, condemnation and execution. But in the humanity of one who came to save, who loved his Father ardently and his own disciples so deeply, these events were not under the serenity of cool calculations. They pierced Jesus' soul. After the Passover meal, Jesus went out to pray.

The gospels tell us that Jesus began "to be greatly distressed and troubled" (Mark 14: 33). He was agitated, unable in the moment to settle the burden pressing upon him. Feeling the urgency of the near future crashing in, Jesus did not want to turn his face to receive that blow. Jesus himself said, "My soul is very sorrowful, even to death" (Mark 14: 34). His very words echo Psalm 6: 2-3[44], which goes on to plead, "Turn, O LORD, deliver my life; save me for the sake of your steadfast love. For in death there is no remembrance of you; in Sheol who will give you praise?" (Ps. 6: 4-5). Jesus knew what was coming and it appalled him.

Jesus had sorrowed over the people's rejection of the mercy he brought. But now something more crept upon him: a sense of his Father's displeasure. He was becoming the wrath bearer. Not just the forgiver of sins, but the reason why his Father could forgive: he was the propitiation for sin. Jesus was taking on the sins of the world as if they were his own. He felt his own repugnance at the human choice for death against the life of God. But worse, he felt his Father's recoiling from the destruction of good creation that is the essence of all sin. "O LORD, rebuke me not in your anger, nor discipline me in your wrath." Jesus engaged in his soul the choice to become sin and receive hell before the powers of evil were allowed to exercise their violent will upon him. As he had said, "I lay down my life for the sheep.... For this reason the Father loves me, because I lay down my life that I may take it up again. No one takes it from me, but I lay it down of my own accord" (John 10: 15, 17-18). Jesus knew that "this charge I have received from my Father" (John 10: 18), but in experience at this hour he could not feel his Father's love and pleasure. The descent into hell had begun.

Oil of the Anointed One

The place where Jesus prayed was the nearby Mount of Olives. This hill is still covered with olive trees today, some of them as old as 900 years, among the most ancient trees on earth. He went to a place on the mountain called Gethsemane, which means literally an "olive press." Here olives were squeezed to yield the precious oil so vital for heating, illuminating and cooking. The base of an olive press is a huge stone basin. An enormous mill stone fit in that bowl. A system of ropes and wood poles allowed the user to roll the stone around the basin. When the great rock bowl was filled with olives, the grinding stone would be rolled over them, crushing the olives with such weight that the oil would seep out. The meat and skins of the olives would get truly pulverized to release the precious oil.[45]

Ancient kings of Israel were anointed with olive oil as a sign of God's selection of them to reign. The word "Messiah," which in Greek is "Christ," literally means the anointed one. The Messiah was the representative of God who was *anointed* by the Spirit to be the savior and ruler of God's people. Of course the Spirit descended on Jesus at his baptism. He got anointed for ministry as the Father declared him to be his beloved Son and the Spirit alighted on him like a dove. But now, in Gethsemane, as Jesus drew near to completing our salvation, Jesus the Messiah would *himself* have to be squeezed. Jesus had to enter the olive press where the weight of the world was upon him. His own soul was crushed by the burden of our sin. Jesus would have to make a deliberate choice to move into the darkness, despair and death of bearing the sin of the world upon himself. Remaining faithful to his mission, Jesus our King was going to be pressed down unto death on the cross.

Death of the Heart

Raniero Cantalamessa considers Gethsemane to reveal the "interior aspect of Jesus' passion: the death of the heart, which precedes and gives meaning to the death of the body.... Gethsemane signals the deepest depression in the passing of Jesus from this world to the Father."[46] Jesus declared that he was sorrowful unto death. What kind of sadness is that? I imagine for Jesus it felt like this:

To be pressed down with grief like an olive under a mill stone. To have the weight of the world on your back and feel like it will crush you, never to rise again. And when it does crush you, not only will you not rise again, but the world will not rise. All will have been in vain. All will be lost. And there will be no one to blame but you. All you wanted, all you prayed for, worked for, and yearned for will be gone. All the power you expended to heal will be for naught. All this world that you tasted with such joy will become ashes in your mouth. Everyone and everything you love will be lost. Forever. But worse, far worse, the presence you have always known is receding. The comforting assurance of your Father's love in your heart that you have felt since infancy is slipping away. You are becoming repugnant to him. He is turning away from you. The emptiness is horrifying. What was full in your soul has evaporated. The solid floor has vanished. Yawning abyss is below. Nothing awaits but endless darkness.[47]

No wonder Jesus recoiled from what lay ahead. He fell on his face and spoke the cry of his soul directly, "My Father, if it be possible, let this cup pass from me." Get me out of this. Save me. Don't leave me. Do this another way. The horror is too much to bear. Abba, take this cup from me.

When all feeling of God's favor was gone, Jesus leaned on the Scriptures. He leaned on the sacred record of what his Father had done in the past. He recalled his baptism and the Father's voice. He recalled his mission. He recalled though he could not feel it, the love which had passed between Father and Son from all eternity. He claimed their shared determination to save the world which had gone bad. "Abba, Father, if it be possible, let this cup pass from me. Nevertheless, not as *I* will, but as *you* will." He prayed in that moment the very words he had taught his disciples to pray, "Our Father, *thy* kingdom come. *Thy* will be done."

The fate of the universe turned on this adamantine will of fidelity. We can imagine how the powers of sin and evil howled inside Jesus' soul. The accumulated rebel shout of every human heart, "Me! My Way!" clamored for him to forget us and save himself. Yet Jesus silenced that roar with what might have been no more than a hoarse whisper, "Nevertheless." The lone human voice of faithfulness reverberated through the cacophony of our rebellion all the way back to Eden. At infinite cost to himself, Jesus answered his Father rightly for us.

In Gethsemane, Jesus made the revolting choice to drink the cup of wrath he did not deserve. The light of the world consented to be extinguished into the deepest darkness. Christ our life stepped into the waters of death and forsakenness in order that we might *pass over* them as safely as passing through dry land. Our innocent

Passover lamb gave himself to be sacrificed for us. The sinless one clasped to himself the contradiction of being made sin. He entered fully the olive press of Gethsemane.

Jesus engaged spiritually the forsakenness on the cross before he was actually arrested and crucified. Gethsemane represented the final temptation to turn from the horror and let the world go to hell instead of himself. He was embracing the sins of the world as his own. He had told his disciples bravely, "The hour is coming . . . when you will be scattered . . . and will leave me alone. Yet I am not alone for the Father is with me" (John 16: 32). Indeed the Father was with him as he had been from all eternity. The Father and Son, bound by the Spirit, enacted the plan of redemption as determined in the counsels of eternity. But the incarnate Son now experienced how in our frailty and finitude, no matter how much we *know* what is going to happen, we cannot be fully prepared for how it actually *feels*. The Father was with Jesus, but to Jesus, the Father was receding with the infinite distance of sin between them.

These words from Hebrews fit the moment. "In the days of his flesh, Jesus offered up prayers and supplications, with loud cries and tears, to him who was able to save him from death, and he was heard because of his reverence. Although he was a son, he learned obedience through what he suffered. And being made perfect, he became the source of eternal salvation to all who obey him" (Heb. 5: 7-9).

After the titanic effort of consecrating his will in Gethsemane, Jesus seemed to shift from being troubled to being at peace. He presented perfect equanimity before the chief priest, the Judean king and the Roman governor. He had crossed the line between active temptation of choice and the peace of resolution. The agony would persist, but it would be clear that Jesus was master even of the powers that bound him.

The Road to Golgotha

As Jesus finished his prayers, soldiers came to Gethsemane to seize him. Led by one of Jesus' own closest disciples, they identified Jesus as Judas kissed him on the cheek. Jesus knew this moment was coming (Mark 14: 18) and he met his arresters head on (Mark 14: 41-42). From his arrest through his crucifixion, Jesus became the object of group scorn, bearing the ridicule due a scapegoat. Francis Spufford imagines the way the onlookers would rise to the occasion of mocking a rejected man, "And just look at him. There's something disgusting about him, don't you think? Something that makes you squirm inside."[48]

Throughout his ministry, Jesus had borne, without losing his head, the transference of the people's hopes to him. Now he had to receive their visceral rejection without losing faith in his Father or his mission. Hours of inquisition followed the arrest: a sham of a trial before the high priest, derisive questions before King Herod, and encounters with Pilate who wanted to release him but bowed to the pressure of group-think in the mob. Finally in the morning, they led Jesus to Golgotha, the Place of the Skull. Mark is the master of understatement, "And they led him out to crucify him" (Mark 15: 20).

So simple to say. One little verb: crucify. But so much involved. Accusation. Arrest. Trial. Condemnation. Beating. Mocking. Parading through the streets before jeering crowds. The stripping off of the clothes to shame the victim and the gawking spectators. The spreading wide of the arms against a rough wood beam. The spike into the ulnar collateral ligament under the thumb and forefinger. Or perhaps in the wrist between the radius and ulna, being careful not to hasten death by severing a vital artery. Feet turned outward, one over the other so a single spike could pin them both under the ankle. The ripping jerk as the victim is hoisted into place. The hours with every breath an agony, drawn only by desperation to breathe.

The long, slow asphyxiation from exhaustion. The physical pain that screamed away coherence. The unity of a human being in body and soul meant that Jesus' corporeal agony witnessed to his soul that he was cursed and justly abandoned. Crucifixion is the cruelest death a government has yet devised.

Gazing through eyes bleary with blood, sweat and tears, Jesus saw the utter despair of Psalm 22 playing out below him. Great was the physical pain. Piercing was the rejection by those he came to save. But worse, worst of all, was the fact that Jesus felt abandoned by his Father in heaven. On the cross, Jesus did not feel the presence he had felt all his life. He who knew the Father so intimately now felt utterly cut off from God. Jesus was driven by the scene below him and the emptiness within him to cry out the saddest prayer in all Scripture, the first verse of Psalm 22:

> My God, my God, why have you forsaken me?
> Mark 15: 34

That's all of the psalm the Gospel writers report Jesus speaking. But to anyone familiar with the psalm, the next lines would have come to mind. They would have been in Jesus' memory and surely in his soul's desperate experience. We are meant to hear what follows:[49]

> Why are you so far from saving me,
>   from the words of my groaning?
> O my God, I cry by day, but you do not answer,
>   and by night, but I find no rest.
> Ps. 22: 1-2

Crying out for comfort, Jesus felt none. Begging for deliverance he was answered by silence from the heavens. It felt to Jesus that his Father had gone over to the side of his enemies. It seemed like God was agreeing with the priests and the scribes after all. They were right. Jesus was wrong. He wasn't a savior, he was a menace.

A fraud. It seemed like God was in collusion with Rome, the devil and all his enemies. As if his Father had said, "Just take him. I don't want him anymore either."

As we noted in chapter one, Jesus' distress on the cross is called the *moment of dereliction*. A derelict building is an abandoned building. No longer fit for human occupancy, the derelict building will be demolished. A derelict person is a hobo, someone who has forsaken normal responsibilities and duties to go wandering on the edges of society. Such a person is bound for the pit. To enter dereliction is to be discarded, to become dumpster material, thrown in the barrel and forgotten. Abandoned without regret.

In these hours, Jesus took to himself the violent reaction that occurs when our self-enthronement is threatened by the claims of God. He drew like a magnet from the crowd the rage (unjustly projected) against God for the consequences of *our* self-idolatry. The God-hatred in the human heart leapt upon him. But Jesus also bore the righteous wrath of God against humanity's destructive rebellion. Jesus became the object of God's final "No!" to our attempts to be God ourselves. He became the meeting place between humanity's rejection of God and God's rejection of *our* rejection of him. These were the hours when Jesus, from both sides, was bearing the sin of the world. The sinless Christ stood in for helpless yet violent, lost yet enraged, sinners. Jesus became the bearer of human and divine wrath. In his pierced body and spurned soul, Jesus was making at-one-ment for the sin of the world. He brought together the estranged parties by taking both our unjust evil and God's just wrath into himself. He was paying for it all. Thus, he was as alone as alone can be.

On the cross, Jesus became sin (2 Cor. 5: 21). As he did in symbolic anticipation in his baptism, now Jesus truly stood in for the sinner *as* a sinner. Though guilty of none of our sin, he received from us all that is abhorrent to his Father. He accepted our deeds, our neglect, our thoughts, our very core of sin as his own, though it sundered the intimacy he had cherished with his Father from all eternity. He went where we should go, alone, in dereliction and cried out, "My God, why have you forsaken me?" For Jesus on the cross, the Father seemed to make no reply except to let it happen. As if he deserved every bit of it.

Whatever else the descent into hell means, it surely means these hours of physical agony amidst spiritual abandonment. And Jesus entered this descent voluntarily and for the purpose of redeeming us. Jesus on the cross descended into the undeserved hell of God-forsakenness to save us. So, the forty-fourth answer in the Heidelberg Catechism gives this as the reason for the descent clause in the creed, "That in my greatest temptations, I may be assured, and wholly comfort myself in this, that my Lord Jesus Christ, by his inexpressible anguish, pain and terrors, which he suffered in his soul upon the cross, and before, hath delivered me from the anguish and torments of hell."

The Trinity on the Cross

We are horrified to witness Jesus' despair at his Father's deliberate refusal to reply to his cries. It seems in the moment the most stunning proof that God is *not* love, and may not even be real. Yet, Christ's disciples through the centuries have by faith also seen another reality occurring during Christ's dying hours. There is an artistic tradition since the middle ages of portraying the Holy Trinity in the crucifixion. The Son is on the cross, but behind him is the Father. The Father's arms hold the beams of the cross as he gazes sadly but resolutely upon the Son's dying. The Spirit, as a dove hovers between the heads of Father and Son, the bond of love between them, cohering even as it is stretched to the extreme.

One of the most famous examples of this symbolism is the Masaccio fresco in the church of Santa Maria Novella in Florence. Painted on a flat wall in 1425, the artist remarkably achieves a three-dimensional affect. Viewers feel as if they are gazing into a chapel inhabited by the three divine persons. The cross looks as if its base is on an altar. Below the altar table is a sarcophagus with a skeleton on top of it. Translated, the words above these bones speak to the viewer, "I once was what you are now, and what I am you also will be." We, the audience alive in this world, are invited to gaze upon our future. Dust will surely come of these bones. The ground will receive, willingly or not, the offering of our corpse.

But the altar above the grave contains another kind of death. The Son willingly gives his life, drawing up the bones of our death into his death. And his defeat, his ignominious death alone, is actually enfolded, by the hovering Spirit's bond, into his Father's loving arms. The Father holds the cross beams. He has not abandoned his Son who nevertheless feels forsaken. Yet he seems to lift the cross with a light touch. Masaccio creates the effect that the Father offers his dying Son to us. His gaze, however, is straight ahead, as if he is too pained to look down at Jesus, or toward us, the viewers, whose plight has demanded such a price. This is tender, fierce, determined love. We can add one more dimension by recalling an ancient tradition that Jesus was crucified above the bones of Adam. Masaccio draws us through our death, through Jesus' death, into the Father's arms and the Triune God's eternal plan of redemption as he creates a new humanity in his Son.

So we understand the Son's forsakenness on the cross as his *experience,* his horribly decimating experience, of abandonment by his Father even though the bond between them was not actually sundered.[50] The union of the Triune persons was not breached, though strained to the limits. Douglas Kelly writes, "Christ's cry of dereliction does not indicate that the Holy Trinity was ever split apart; for that to happen, everything would collapse into nonbeing, for God would have denied who he is, and his character is the stability of the universe."[51]

In the historic understanding of *perichoresis,* the interpenetration of the three persons of the Triune God, it is said that wherever one person of the Trinity may be found, there are the others. In fact, the Father is everything the Son is except that he is *not* the Son; the Son is all the Holy Spirit is except that he is *not* the Spirit, and so forth in all the relations. There is only "distance" between them insofar as love between persons requires someone who is not oneself in order to love. This distance between the persons is ordinarily not observable by us in revelation. But on the cross, the unity and the distinction of the persons were both strained and exposed. The "distance" that makes the divine persons three distinct persons in union rather than an undifferentiated oneness was stretched to the maximum limit.

The eternal Son of God undertook the journey of the descent in all its ever more demanding stages to save us. But this was a work of the divine counsel of Father, Son and Holy Spirit. To put it another way, by the terms of the covenant of redemption the Triune God himself designed, the Father had to close his ears to his Son's cries. Can we possibly calculate the grief of the Father whose everlasting delight has been to answer his Son then going silent in the hours of his greatest suffering? By these covenant terms, the Son had to enter dereliction to bear our sins. And the Spirit, who is personally the Love between Father and Son, whom we know can be grieved (Eph. 4: 30), willingly bore the strain of holding the Lover and the Beloved together while our sin stood starkly between them.

Father Raniero goes to the heart of the matter with his usual poignant clarity,

> Therefore, the heavenly Father and his Son, Jesus, were together in the passion and together on the cross. More than to the wooden arms of the cross, Jesus was nailed to his Father's arms or, as it were, to his will. Just as it is in eternity it is from the unutterable and joyful embrace between the Father and the Son that the Holy Spirit proceeds—the gift of their mutual love— so now and for all time, it is from that painful embrace

of the Father and Son on the cross that the Holy Spirit flows—the gift of both of them for us.[52]

The pictorial typology of centuries of Christian art reveals a deep theological truth. Jesus could be depicted as nailed to his Father's arms because he was, from everlasting bliss through the utter hell of the cross, bolted to his Father's will in mutual love by the blessed Holy Spirit.

Into Your Hands

The gospels record seven sayings from Jesus on the cross, two of them quotations from the psalms. We do not know the exact order in which he said them. But it does seem clear that his cry, "My God, why have you forsaken me?" was not his final word. Just before he died, Jesus said "Father, into your hands I commit my spirit" (Luke 23: 46, quoting Ps. 31: 5). For some, this prayer indicates that Jesus experienced a restoration of his fellowship with his Father.[53] He knew the offering of his life as atonement was accepted and he could die in peace. I think we will see after our exploration of Holy Saturday that it is more consistent to consider that Jesus remained under dereliction all the way through his death.[54] Thus, praying Psalm 31 would be an act of sheer faithfulness flung against the wall of the Father's resolutely turned back. This would mean that faced with utter nothingness, with no trace of his Father to be found, Jesus yet acted in fidelity and trust. As we noted in Chapter 1, Torrance considers this to be the climactic moment in the lifelong fidelity of Jesus through which he had been remaking our humanity. On the cross, under abandonment, Christ was restructuring our humanity from faithlessness to fidelity.[55] This moment thus connects to Paul's glorious declaration that in Christ, we are a new creation (2 Cor. 5: 17).

In this chapter, we have looked at events too deep and too

high for us. Although invited by Scripture to gaze, we yet have the feeling of having invaded the privacy of the intimate relationship that is the Triune God. Jesus' heartbreak is so acute that we feel like voyeurs for beholding it. These events are not business transactions. The faith required of Jesus to commit himself to his Father at the last was not born of some easy sense that the end of the play was already a given. He was not merely acting out a character whose role did not touch his real being. His faith rose through the excruciating pain of true flesh, and the shattered soul of a real man. Such wondrous love summons a reply of love.

Doxological Treasure

The 17th Anglican poet and priest, George Herbert wrote down a remarkable prayer to be offered before he began a sermon. In this excerpt, we hear Herbert contemplating the great paradox that to save us, God, who cannot die, *did* die.

> You have exalted your mercy above all things and you have made our salvation, not our punishment, to be your glory: so that then where sin abounded, not death, but grace *superabounded.*

> Accordingly, when we had sinned beyond any help in heaven or earth, then you said, Lo, I come!

> Then did the Lord of life, unable himself to die, contrive to do it.

> He took flesh, he wept, he died; for his enemies he died; even for those that derided him then, and still despise him.

Blessed Saviour! Many waters could not quench your love! Nor no pit overwhelm it. But though the streams of your blood were current through darkness, grave and hell; yet by these your conflicts, and seemingly hazards, you did rise triumphant, and therein made us victorious.[56]

We cannot grasp that God, who is life in himself, could possibly die. Death does not fit any categories of divinity. Yet, our situation was dire: we had sinned beyond any known help in heaven or earth. So the eternal Son suited up in our flesh. "Lo, I come!" he said as he descended to us. The eternal God worked out a way to die for us— he took up flesh that could be pierced and could expire. Jesus came to make all things new (Rev. 21: 5), but that required an impossible feat. "Then did the Lord of life, unable himself to die, contrive to do it." The Triune God became man to die in order to make us live. God by definition cannot die, but he did. And he died in such a way that his blood ran like a life-giving stream "through darkness, grave and hell." He descended into death that we might live.

We turn now to the silent Sabbath of Holy Saturday.

~ 5 ~

DEAD STOP SATURDAY

We would like to be done with it. We want his suffering to stop. Viscerally, we crave resurrection morning to arrive at 3:01 Friday afternoon to restore Jesus. Once in a study, the discussion turned to the question of what happened to Jesus after he died. A woman with a loving mother's heart said, "I just want it to be over for him. I can't stand to think that after the horrible cross his pain could continue in any way." Indeed, if we let through our defenses even a smidgeon of Golgotha, we share her yearning. Moreover, theologically, we get anxious that anything might need to be added to the sufficiency of the sacrifice of Jesus on the cross. "It is finished," (John 19: 30) surely means completion.[57] Also, we naturally seek a punctiliar moment about which we can say, "There! That's where and when he saved us. With that exact word at that precise moment."

But that is not how the gospel narrative was written. Jesus did not just skim death, he descended fully into it. The cross was not a single moment but a series of agonizing moments across those dreadful three hours. Every one of them was vital to the sacrificial work of Jesus on our behalf. For, until he actually died, at any of those moments Jesus could have called a halt (Matt. 26: 53), sparing his bodily life but killing our hope for eternal life. Thus, each searing second represented a deliberate choice to obey his Father as he loved us unto death.

As well, that time on the cross remains integrally connected to what preceded. Gethsemane, the trials before the chief priests and Pilate, and the stumbling, forced march to the cross are each and all essential to the crucifixion. Go back further, and we see that every moment of Jesus' sinless life of perfect fidelity to the Father and filial love to all whom he encountered are the only reasons the cross can "work" as an atoning sacrifice. But those years of ministry require the mystery of the incarnation itself and the ensuing hidden years of growth and learning. Calvin eloquently noted that "the whole course of his obedience" is necessary to our salvation.[58]

So far we have traced Christ's great transit of mercy as we followed the series of his descents leading to the cross. We dare not stop telling the story of descent now! The next twenty-seven to thirty-nine hours will be crucial to Jesus' salvific work.[59] We will be tempted, as the church has ever been, to collapse this gap of Holy Saturday's silence into the victory shouts of Easter morning. The tension is terrible, but we will hold it a chapter longer. Theology must remain, as a lady-in-waiting, in service to the sacred narrative.

Death After Dying

They took his body down from the cross and wrapped it in a burial shroud. The fine linen blotted the blood, sweat and dirt on the corpse. It served as a clean, peaceful wrapping, shrouding the chaotic wounds of the violence that spoiled his precious flesh. Then Joseph of Arimathea placed Jesus' body "in his own new tomb, which he had cut in the rock. And he rolled a great stone to the entrance of the tomb and went away" (Matt. 27: 60). He left because sunset approached and Sabbath laws forbade further work. But actually there was nothing more to be done anyway. They walked away because Jesus had expired. His voice was stilled and his mission terminated. His disciples knew where his body was between Good Friday afternoon and Easter Sunday: inert, fixed and sealed by rock in rock. Just like it would have happened to anyone else in that day.

His spirit had passed beyond our sight. Gone beyond our ken, Jesus' spirit could not be followed by anyone remaining in the world. He followed the pattern of every other human death. To use Laufer's pithy phrase, Jesus was "incarnate unto death."[60] Though his spirit was sundered from his body, he continued in the normal human trajectory of death. Jesus entered Sheol/Hades, the realm of departed spirits, the state of the dead.

The next question concerns the quality of that sojourn among the dead. Jesus died in defeat. But that death was also his triumph. So was he in the realm of departed spirits as someone crushed and still covered in shame? Or was he simply resting from his labors while a Sabbath unfolded in the daylight world?[61] Or did he arrive in Sheol as the conqueror come to liberate the faithful dead? Was it some combination of all three? The paradox of victorious defeat lies at the heart of the gospel. So as we explore the silence in our world during the Sabbath of Holy Saturday, we know we are examining cords that cannot finally be untwined. The events of the Triduum, the three days from Gethsemane to Easter morning, are woven together with forsakenness and restoration, disgrace and triumph, death and life in a union that always holds them together.

Paul embraced this paradox. Surely he shocked his readers who would have been all too familiar with the shame crucifixion brought not only to the victim but to his family and followers as well. These executions utterly decimated any would-be challengers to Rome. Yet Paul writes that by the cross, God actually "disarmed the rulers and authorities and put them to open shame, by triumphing over them in [Christ]" (Col. 2: 15). This death, which always brought generations of disgrace to the families of the crucified, rebounded against the powers who killed Jesus. Hebrews declares this same paradox that "through death he might destroy the one who has the power of death" (Heb. 2: 14). So, the heart of our faith holds this startling reversal that from utter humiliation came complete victory. We hold together the crucified conqueror and the nail pierced risen one in Revelation's image of the Lamb who stands victorious, yet appears as one slain (Rev. 5: 6).

But was Jesus' own awareness of his triumph *immediate* upon death? Jesus had passed beyond earthly choice, his obedience complete. So had Jesus now passed beyond any volition into the passivity of the dead? Or was he worshiping in his Father's presence? Was the triumph we know he had on Easter actually experienced by Jesus right after his death? Or did the humiliation entered via his torturous crucifixion continue a while in the realm of the dead? Was there a time, in that realm out of time, *after* the cross when Jesus continued to perceive separation from his Father?

In this section, I'd like to try on the possibility that in descending fully into our death, Jesus on Holy Saturday was not yet restored to experiencing the joy of his relationship with the Father. Three reasons undergird my conjecture: 1) His death meant *being* dead. 2) Jesus predicted a sojourn among the dead akin to that of all people. 3) A Jesus rejoicing on Holy Saturday contradicts the despair in which he left his disciples.

1) For as long as he lived on the cross, Jesus was *not* dead. Therefore he was not fully undergoing the perception of total abandonment that is separation from the Father, the due consequence of sin. Think of it: in being dead, Jesus experienced something other, indeed worse, than he did on the horrible cross. For even in agony, a body is yet alive. There is a goodness in embodied life that mitigates utter forsakenness, no matter how tortured such life may be. Even while we perish, the flesh tries to repair itself, the heart beats, and the lungs strain for breath. All these are signs of life and light over against the dark void. By contrast, the disembodied soul loses the sensations that assure one of existence. Gone is the witness, even in pain, that a live body makes to the goodness of a Creator. Moreover, on the cross, Jesus yet knew human presence. He heard human voices, even if they mocked him. He saw that Mary and John stood by, and he spoke to them (John 19: 26-27). Thus, he was not utterly alone for Jesus on the cross had, albeit scant, a human comfort when he did not have a divine one. But in

death, interaction with other humans ceased. An essential quality of being dead before the work of Christ was aloneness.

2) Jesus expected that after his death on the cross, his soul would enter the realm of departed spirits like other humans. We recall his prediction in Matthew 12 that just as Jonah spent three days and nights in the belly of the great fish, so Jesus would spend three days and nights in the heart of the earth. Jesus' identification with Jonah's journey warrants our linking Jonah's prayer with Jesus' own prayers. Praying Jonah's prayer, Jesus would have anticipated sharing Jonah's fate on Holy Saturday. The words would resonate for what he knew was coming. "You cast me into the deep" (Jon. 2: 3). Jesus understood the popular metaphors. One can walk without hindrance into the realm of death. Its gates are open. But as soon as a victim crosses the threshold, the unbreakable bars of Sheol's gates close behind him. "I went down to the land whose bars closed upon me forever" (Jon. 2: 6). This is a place beyond the sight of the living, with deeper depths than can be plumbed and farther reaches than can be traversed by the people of earth. Regarding the LORD, it felt to the dead, before Christ's work was complete, as if "I am driven away from your sight" (Jon. 2: 4). Jonah felt profoundly cut off as he plummeted to the bottom of the sea, not only because he thought he would die, but because he was dying in disobedience. He was dying as a result of his flight from enacting the will of God he knew to do. Thus he sank in disgrace and condemnation. Even more so, Jesus, bearing the sins of the world, fell from the agony of the cross into the abyss of deathly separation from his Father. Perhaps this condition felt like it would last forever. Praying this prayer ahead of his death, Jesus would have prepared for the plunge. Jesus purposed to answer from the abyss, without a shred of confirming evidence, the hope Jonah expressed *after* his rescue, "Yet I shall again look upon your holy temple" (Jon. 2: 4).

3) Beyond Jesus' own identification with Jonah, another strong reason to believe that Jesus' sojourn in Sheol was not immediately triumphant arises when we consider what was going on "up here"

on Holy Saturday. Jesus' disciples were frightened, gathered behind locked doors (John 20: 19). They were grieved (Luke 24: 17) and all hope that Jesus was the redeemer was now in the past (Luke 24: 21). Their very incredulity on Sunday, upon hearing that the women had seen Jesus (Luke 24: 11), indicates that on Saturday they did *not* remember, or in remembering did not believe, Jesus' predictions of his resurrection. The Romans and the religious officials appeared to have triumphed. God's visitation of his people (Luke 1: 68), if it had ever happened, was decidedly over, with little to show for it. The disciples had given up everything to follow Jesus and now they had lost him and their sacrifice seemed in vain.

Just as Jesus allowed his friends to wait in mourning before he raised Lazarus, so now his disciples had to wait without hope on the Saturday between cross and resurrection. It is instructive to recall the way in which Jesus engaged that interval with Lazarus. When Jesus saw the people mourning over his deceased friend, he was "deeply moved in his spirit and greatly troubled" (John 11: 33). He wept even though he knew he would soon raise Lazarus. Jesus expressed deep empathy with us throughout his days among us. Does it match the character of our Lord then, to consider his spirit dancing in triumphant reception before his Father while leaving those he came to save in utter despair here below? Could he possibly be rejoicing if he were, without deep purpose or even necessity, delaying a return to his weeping beloved ones? The fact is that it is just as much conjecture to consider Jesus exulting in spirit on Holy Saturday while his disciples wept as it is to consider that he remained under the power of death in human spirit as well as body.[62]

Jesus' absence on Holy Saturday demanded a waiting from his disciples and continues to demand a waiting from us as we mark the events of Holy Week. All the work of the incarnate Redeemer in his disciples' lives came to a dead stop in this world. This indicates a full stop for Jesus as well, even though we cannot directly see what Jesus was doing, or not doing, in the hiatus of Holy Saturday. The correspondence between Jesus' journey of descent and the life of his people would lead us to reasonable conjecture even when we cannot see the realm beyond: Jesus remained silent in Sabbath rest during Holy Saturday. He had won victory on the cross, but he was not yet recalled to life in the world, nor yet called to exult in that triumph below.

Was Sheol a Hell for Jesus?

We now consider the quality of this passivity for Jesus. Could it have been a continuing sense of forsakenness? If so, that means that when the intensity of the physical pain vanished in death, the spiritual void of abandonment and failure in his mission would have loomed before Jesus. The nerve endings screaming in pain can hope for pain's end. The soul must wait without hope of cessation. Balthasar's pioneering work on Holy Saturday takes us deep into the meaning of this hiatus between Good Friday and Easter.[63] Balthasar insists that the spirit of Jesus went into the Sheol of the Old Testament, just like any other person.[64] He entered into solidarity with all the dead because he became like them. But to Balthasar, Jesus' experience of death in Sheol also exceeded that of anyone else. Jesus is the Son of God who took up our humanity to fulfill the Triune mission of reconciling us to God. As the God-man, he underwent a deeper fall beneath the power of death, knowing a loneliness, darkness and despair beyond that experienced by even the most sinful soul.[65] He went to the place of death, the ultimate solitary confinement, in such a way that through his own utter aloneness, he *brothered* all the dead.

Balthasar writes that a theology of Holy Saturday consists of:

> something unique, expressed in the 'realisation' of all Godlessness, of all the sins of the world, now experienced as agony and a sinking down into the 'second death' or 'second chaos', outside of the world

81

ordained from the beginning by God. And so it is really God who assumes what is radically contrary to the divine, what is eternally reprobated by God, in the form of the supreme obedience of the Son towards the Father. . . .[66]

We know that Jesus went to the dead as the one who conquered sin and death by his complete offering of himself unto death as the pure Lamb of God. Against every appearance in the world at 3 p.m. on Good Friday, Jesus triumphed as he died on the cross. That is when Satan was defeated. No further combat in Hades was required. But Balthasar asserts that during Holy Saturday Jesus did not get to behold his victory. He went to the dead as the man accursed for dying on a tree (Gal. 3: 13), who had become sin (2 Cor. 5: 21) as he bore the sin of the world. That horror was what he knew in Hades.

The Vision of Death

While some of the dead had lived with faith in a Redeemer, and therefore waited in the gloom with a glimmer of hope, for Balthasar, Jesus experienced no such hope. The news of Jesus' victory by his once-for-all triumph of the cross was withheld from him during Holy Saturday. All that appeared before him was unending death. The absolute loneliness that is the result of sin-in-itself gripped the soul of Jesus.

Into Holy Saturday Balthasar daringly brings the vision of death. Jesus did not experience the restoration of his Father's favor before the resurrection. Rather, he beheld utter defeat. Another psalm of David resonates here: "For the enemy has pursued my soul; he has crushed my life into the ground; he has made me sit in darkness like those long dead. Therefore, my spirit faints within me; my heart within me is appalled" (Ps. 143: 3-4). Because Jesus had become identified with our sin, the enemy was—*in Jesus' immediate experience of the moment*—not only the raging human and demonic powers, but also his Father himself who condemned Jesus to this fate. The dead-stop finality of it appalled Christ's soul.

Balthasar, however, presses even farther. He asserts that Jesus had a vision of sin itself, in its horrifying objectivity and final conclusion. He beheld the ultimate result of man's "No" to God echoing into eternity. All of this could have been included in Jesus' vision of death before he knew he had won, when he perceived only utter failure in his mission to redeem a lost world. Christ's triumph on the cross came through death, and while in Sheol, Jesus knew only the deathly part of the cross, "the absolute emptying of life which he knew as the Dead One."[67]

David Lauber lucidly summarizes the position of Balthasar:

> The victory over sin wrought by his sacrificial death was kept from Jesus Christ in the descent into hell. The descent into hell is the product of Jesus' pure obedience, obedience that persists even in the face of utter hopelessness and abandonment—in the face of everything that is in opposition to God. . . . The ultimate outcome of this obedience is kept from Jesus, and this makes his obedience all the more pure, and his death and descent into hell truly redemptive. It is only by genuinely experiencing the utter hopelessness of the abandonment, forsakenness, and separation from God, which is the consequence of sin, that Jesus can destroy sin and restore hope to humanity.[68]

In this view, then, Holy Saturday was the day when it was profoundly *not* all right for Jesus or his disciples. What we saw in this world was seeing in the mirror darkly, a shadow of the vision of death Christ beheld.

Deeper and Farther: Comprehending our Death

The purpose for Jesus undergoing such a vision on Holy Saturday as Balthasar proposes was, of course, our redemption from the condemnation of sin and the power of death. Spatial language helps us here. Jesus in Sheol sank deeper under death, with all its consequences as the wages of sin (Rom. 6: 23), than any human has gone. He was exiled farther away from awareness of his Father than any prodigal has ever run. And yet he remained faithful, trusting the Father he could not sense. So Job's words, "Though he slay me, yet will I trust in him," (Job 13: 15, KJV) found their deepest meaning through Jesus on Holy Saturday.

The LORD's own description of his wrath against our rebellion directs us to this interpretation: "For a fire is kindled by my anger, and it burns to the depths of Sheol, devours the earth and its increase, and sets on fire the foundations of the mountains" (Deut. 32: 22). Jesus had to go to the very roots not only of the earth but of the spiritual realm in order to extinguish the fire at its source. For human sin struck at the root of God's good creation. Our poison courses through the decay in the world (Rom. 8: 21). We stretch as far with our self-assertion as we are able into the universe, and were not the Tree of Life closed off from us (Gen. 3: 24) we would have extended our sin into eternity. To be cleansed from the root up, to have our heart recreated and life restored, we needed a redemption that plumbed to the foundation, the beginning, of our creation. We required the quenching of the fires burning under all our death as, left unchecked and to our own devices, our in-turned souls would consume themselves forever.

So Jesus in Sheol *comprehended* our death. He got all the way around it. He died "beneath" our death and thereby got his "hands" around our lethal problem. Jesus circumscribed our sin and its consequences by taking on more, plunging farther, dying deeper, being crushed finer—the metaphors pile up but still cannot measure the immeasurable depths to which he went in order to offer us an embrace that contains us entirely and heals us from within. Jesus in his infinite capacity as the God-man took upon himself sin-in-itself and the absolute death to which it leads.

In descending to the dead, Christ encompasses the realm of the dead. He comprehends it, so that all death is now contained within his experience of being dead and then being raised. In this way, Psalm 95 applies to him, "For the LORD is a great God and a great King above all gods. In his hand are the depths of the earth; the heights of the mountains are his also" (Ps. 95: 3-4). All the deeps of the earth now fit in his nail-pierced palm. We sang as children, "He's got the whole world in his hands." But we never knew just how big those hands must be. For little did we know that by his descent, Jesus now holds the entire depths of Sheol. He in himself contains the abyss and has brought light into it for all who will trust him. He has gathered up all our dying. He has swallowed all our sinning. He has made them his own that we might be made his own.

No Further Suffering than the Cross

By now a keen objection may have arisen to Balthasar's idea of Holy Saturday as an event of Jesus' descent into the vision of death that is hell. It seems to imply that further suffering than the cross was necessary for our salvation. Was the crucifixion not enough? Of course it was. As we noted last chapter, there was no actual, or ontological, sundering in the Triune God. Jesus *experienced* forsakenness in the depths of his soul, though he was not, at the level of God's very being, ever separated from his Father. Further, the event of Jesus offering his life for us occurred once and for all. He need never make that sacrifice again. As the *Westminster Confession* in my tradition asserts, the Triune God made "through the mediation and sacrifice of the Lord Jesus Christ, a way of life and salvation, sufficient for and adapted to the whole lost race of man."[69] But we realize that part of dying includes the *being dead*. God did not resurrect Jesus straight from the cross. His sojourn in Sheol was not further suffering but a necessary, foreknown component of his dying.

Indeed, Balthasar affirms that Jesus' going to the dead was not "a new activity, distinct from the first." Rather it was the outworking of the "fundamentally finished" sacrifice on the cross.[70] Lauber explains:

> We must stress that Balthasar does not suggest that the sacrificial death on Good Friday is somehow inadequate and incomplete, and is therefore in need of the descent into hell in order to be salvific. Rather, Good Friday and Holy Saturday are two distinct but inseparable elements of Jesus Christ's passion. . . . On Holy Saturday Christ is emptied of all activity, becomes completely passive, as in complete solidarity with the dead. This solidarity includes isolation, loneliness and utter passivity. The descent into hell demonstrates . . . the extremity of his self-giving and the unbroken character of his obedience.[71]

The cross was a complete victory, but it does not exist apart from Jesus' previous life of faithfulness nor from the hiatus of Holy Saturday. Neither would the cross be effective without Jesus' resurrection and his ascension into heaven. What Balthasar asserts is that just as Jesus entered solidarity with those he came to save in his incarnation, so he remained in solidarity with us through death. He engaged being dead as one of us, and yet, because he is also the Creator God, he could take on the full effects of death, substituting himself on our behalf.

Is Balthasar correct? He certainly is compelling. Five hundred years earlier, Calvin directed our attention to the cross as a place where Christ descended into hell. Amidst the escalating horrors of the twentieth century, Balthasar pried open space for Holy Saturday to express the Son of God's remaining with us in redemptive forsakenness. Over time, I suspect Balthasar's innovative views will enter our discussions in a moderated form, such as those of Benedict (which we will consider in chapter 7). Certainly one does not have to comprehend or accept all of his massive theological project to appreciate his contribution. He keeps us in pace with the journey Jesus undertook. Holy Saturday was the Great Sabbath in Jesus' transit of mercy. Having descended fully into our death, he waited for the resurrection by which he would raise us with him into life.

Of course, we cannot finally fill in all the content of this narrative blank in the gospel records.[72] We cannot know without question what happened in the interval of Holy Saturday. But by following the trajectory of Jesus' descent from his incarnation, we can trace with some confidence his path to the dead. Though we cannot in this world speak fully of what occurred in the other realm, we do know Jesus descended below the deepest just anger evoked by human sin. And he did it in order to bring us into the freedom of a just forgiveness. He went further away from our Father than we can go in order to bring us back filially and legally, forensically and relationally, to be reconciled eternally to our Father. He let death pile him deeper than any soul had gone, in order that no soul now need sink so low.

Doxological Treasure: New Answers to Rhetorical Questions

Psalm 88 is the most hopeless of all the psalms. The psalmist felt so forsaken by God as to be already in Sheol. He felt like one cut loose from God by God, then dumped into the pit of the dead. Unlike other laments, this psalm ends not with hope but with the words, "Darkness has become my only companion" (Ps. 88: 18, alternate ESV translation). As such, it makes a fitting Holy Saturday prayer for Jesus. We hear lyrics for Christ's experience of Sheol as the hellish vision of death:

> For my soul is full of troubles,
>   and my life draws near to Sheol.
> I am counted among those who go down to the pit;
>   I am a man who has no strength,
> like one set loose among the dead,
>   like the slain that lie in the grave,
> like those whom you remember no more,
>   for they are cut off from your hand.
> You have put me in the depths of the pit,
>   in the regions dark and deep.
> Your wrath lies heavy upon me,
>   and you overwhelm me with all your waves.
>
> You have caused my companions to shun me;
>   you have made me a horror to them.
> I am shut in so that I cannot escape;
>   my eye grows dim through sorrow.
>   Ps. 88: 3-9

These are the prayers of a man with no present hope. He is the lowest of the low, rejected by God and man. To his experience, both regard him now as a pariah. The very presence of this psalm gives us insight into the condemnation and even the being dead of the one who came to identify fully with us, so that he might save us completely from the inside out. This psalm expresses total despair.

And yet. And yet, with Jesus, the turn toward hope is actually contained within this most dire lament. The second half of the psalm contains a series of questions. Throughout the centuries of this psalm's use, the answer to each question would ever have been a resounding "No!" But as we move toward exploring Jesus' resurrection, we begin daring to hear the answer of "Yes" coming from the depths of his soul:

> Do you work wonders for the dead?
> > Do the departed rise up to praise you?
> Is your steadfast love declared in the grave,
> > or your faithfulness in Abaddon?
> Are your wonders known in the darkness,
> > or your righteousness in the land of forgetfulness?
> > > Ps. 88: 10-12

No one in history could have answered in the affirmative. Certainly no one on Holy Saturday would ever have ventured a "Yes" in contradiction to the devastation of Jesus' execution. The endless day of atheism seemed to have dawned. Nietzsche did not invent his own phrase, for on Holy Saturday the disciples felt, "God is dead and we killed him."[73] We put the beautiful savior, the glorious Son of God on the foulest discard pile. But as Saturday turned to Sunday, a new word would be spoken. The Father would indeed work wonders among the dead. He would declare that his steadfast love for his Son had never wavered, not once. In the place of destruction, the news would dawn in Jesus' spirit that the faithfulness between the Father and the Son had triumphed over all the rending evil. For the Spirit would be sent to make a sunrise, enabling the firstborn from the dead to step into the dawn of a world remade.

~ 6 ~

SUNDAY BEFORE SUNRISE

The arc of the savior's descent ended with a splash into the bottomless sea of death. His great transit of mercy took him beneath the depths of all our dying. He dropped out of his body, out of our time, out of any place we know, still unaware of his Father's favor or his victory over sin. Saturday marked the farthest reach of his descent. By dawn on Easter Sunday, though, Jesus was afoot in our world, risen in a body no longer dead, but not merely resuscitated. He rose in a body transformed from subjection to decay (Rom. 8: 21) into "a heavenly dwelling" (2 Cor. 5: 2). He entered an embodiment rigged out for eternity.

For centuries, the church has heard the voice of Christ in Psalm 139. David not only articulated his own experience of the LORD's continuing presence, he scripted a prayer for Jesus' journey to and from the realm of the dead. "Where shall I go from your Spirit? Or where shall I flee from your presence? If I ascend to heaven, you are there! If I make my bed in Sheol, you are there!" (Ps. 139: 7-8). The lonely Sabbath in Sheol turned out *not* to be abandonment. So the church let vs. 18 be the grateful words of the rising Jesus. And on Easter, early in the liturgy, Christ's people repeat it for him:

> I awake, and I am still with you, alleluia. You lay your hand upon me, alleluia.[74]

David's song wondered at the mystery of returning from sleep, from the daily journey into unconsciousness, where one has no control, and finding that the LORD had been watching over him the whole time. Jesus rejoiced, however, that through that deeper sleep of death, he had not, as he feared, been forgotten. Jesus in resurrection awoke to the discovery that he had never been sundered from his Father. [75] The rupture occurred only in his vision and awareness, though his "mere" experience exceeds any pain the rest of us have undergone. But ontologically, in reality, the "forsaking" Father and the "forsaken" Son remained united by the everlasting bond of the Spirit between them. [76] This had all been part of the plan. Now, though weeping had endured for a seemingly endless night, joy had risen with the sun on Easter morning (Ps. 30: 5).

At the resurrection, the Father vindicated the innocence of his Son, countermanding the unjust verdict of humanity that he was worthy of death. How do we imagine this occurring? Did the voice of the Father's declaration thunder throughout the realm of the dead, with a resounding "No!" to our petulant judgment, a concussive "Not Guilty!" to our verdict against him? Or did his Spirit rush toward the Son, like the Father in the parable hitching up his robes and running down the road to welcome home the prodigal? Then perhaps a raucous party ensued in heaven. Or, as Cantalamessa suggests, did the Father send his Spirit softly, as one waking a child from sleep?[77] In this case, the return to life was a gentle rousing, full of tenderness as the Son awoke to the lifted countenance of his Father's love.

The three Marys met the risen Jesus shortly after dawn (Matt. 28: 9). But the first day of the week had begun at sundown the night before. So when, by our reckoning of time, did Jesus get recalled to life? Were there moments, or hours, when the soul of Jesus rose from the stasis of Sheol but did not yet return to his body? Could this be the "time" in which Jesus was "made alive in the spirit in which he proclaimed to the spirits in prison" (1 Pet. 3: 19)? Centuries of interpretation read this passage as pertaining to Jesus' sojourn in Sheol before Easter dawn: "the gospel was preached even to those who are dead" (1 Pet. 4: 6). Much contemporary exegesis now disputes the traditional meaning,[78] but even without the definitive undergirding of this passage, we can inquire if the trajectory of Jesus' dying and rising includes implications for those who had died before him as well as those yet to be.

Binding the Strong Man

The structure of the cosmos changed with the resurrection of Jesus. The very nature of death itself was altered as he rose. Previously, every departed spirit went to Sheol/Hades, the realm of the dead.[79] Now, Jesus has overcome death. He declares, "Fear not, I am the first and the last, and the living one. I died, and behold I am alive forevermore, and I have the keys of Death and Hades" (Rev. 1: 17-18). The cells of Hades are now unlocked. The curse of death no longer determines the destiny of the spirit. Those who belong to Christ skip Sheol.[80] This is why, while we recognize the difficulties in too literally interpreting apocalyptic visions, John the Revelator saw the spirits of the martyrs standing before the throne of the lamb, singing his praises (Rev. 7: 9-12, 15: 2-4). Before the resurrection of the body, before the new heavens and the new earth descend, the souls belonging to Christ are already in his presence. Thus, Paul declares that "to depart" is "to be with Christ," and that to be away from this mortal body is to be "home with the Lord," even before the last trumpet (2 Cor. 5: 6, 1 Cor. 15: 52). After death, we will await the full resurrection of our bodies, but we will not be in a shadowy, lonely realm. We shall be with our savior.[81] Our destiny in Christ is now upward.

Moreover, Jesus' resurrection meant his victory over Satan. This was the binding of the strong man. Jesus plundered the evil one in the very "place" where the evil one's power seemed most evident, the realm of death. Now Sheol was never meant to be considered Satan's personal kingdom, a place where he presides and enacts his will against human souls. The Triune God has ever and will ever remain Lord of both the living and the dead (Rom. 14: 9). But, because the evil one from the beginning tempted humankind into the sin that led to our dying spiritually and physically, death has ever been associated with his power. So Hebrews declares that Jesus shared in our flesh and blood in order "that through death he might destroy the one who has the power of death, that is, the devil, and deliver all those who through fear of death were subject to lifelong slavery" (Heb. 2: 14-15).

Satan never had the actual, ultimate power of life and death. Such belongs to God alone. But his temptations led to our sin which led to our death as the promised consequence. And his continuing accusations lead people to despair of any hope for right standing before God and thus of any expectation but condemnation following death. Jesus in his dying took away the sin of the world. The accusations against us no longer have any grounds. We now have "an advocate with the Father, Jesus Christ the righteous. He is the propitiation for our sins, and not for ours only but also for the sins of the whole world" (1 John 2: 1-2). Our advocate silences the accusations as we trust in the redemption he has won for us. He gives us the answer to all condemnation in his thrilling words, "Because I live, you also will live" (John 14: 19). This is the basis for the ancient, triumphant Easter declaration, "Christ is risen from the dead, trampling down death by death, and bestowing life on those in the tombs."[82]

The Last Adam

In two tantalizing places, Paul introduces the understanding that Jesus represented a new kind of man.[83] In 1 Corinthians 15, Paul writes, "The first man Adam became a living being; the last Adam became a life-giving spirit" (v. 45). He picks up the imagery of Genesis 2: 7 in which "the LORD God formed the man of dust from the ground and breathed into his nostrils the breath of life, and man became a living creature." The word *Adam* is related to the Hebrew word for dust. The stuff of the man was of the earth. He was made spiritual, alive and conscious, by the Spirit, or breath, of God. Adam, with Eve, had the joyful mandate, accompanied with the ability, to reproduce and fill the earth (Gen. 1: 28). But since the fall, all life on earth has been destined to die. Man cannot reproduce himself into embodied, everlasting life. Natural man returns to the dust. With this first Adam, Paul contrasts Jesus who is the last Adam, the Adam that partakes of the *eschaton*, the final intention of God for his creation. This last Adam represents humanity flourishing in the Kingdom of God. Jesus is man as intended, "the image of the invisible God, the firstborn of all creation" (Col. 1: 15). So Jesus himself declared, "As the Father raises the dead and gives them life, so also the Son gives life. . . . For as the Father has life in himself, so he has granted the Son also to have life in himself" (John 5: 21, 26). The resurrected Son is not only alive for himself, but he can give eternal life to all who are joined to him by the Spirit. Now Jesus the last Adam is multiplying the image of God on earth through remade men and women as he pours out his Spirit when the gospel is preached. Multitudes now partake of his resurrection life, entering a new humanity in Jesus. So Paul writes, "If anyone is in Christ, he is a new creation" (2 Cor. 5: 17).

In Romans, Paul draws out the contrast between these Adams, particularly in relationship to our justification. The first Adam sinned, introducing universal death: ". . . sin came into the world through one man, and death through sin, and so death spread to all men because all sinned" (Rom. 5: 12). But the new Adam, Jesus, lived righteousness and fidelity from within our humanity. Throughout "the whole course of his obedience,"[84] Jesus kept the law and remained faithful to his Father. So, "if, because of one man's trespass, death reigned through that one man, much more will those who receive the abundance of grace and the free gift of righteousness reign in life through the one man Jesus Christ"

(Rom. 5: 17). In the first Adam, "sin reigned in death" but in the last Adam, "grace also might reign through righteousness leading to eternal life through Jesus Christ our Lord" (Rom. 5: 21).

Anglican theologian Michael Reeves clearly draws out the implications of the two Adams:

> Have you ever noticed that when Paul writes of Adam and Christ, he writes as if they were the only men in the world, as if no others existed? That was the big picture of humanity for Paul. It is not that humanity is a vast throng of disconnected individuals. Adam and Christ are *the* two men: the heads, the firstfruits of the old and the new human race. Each one of us is merely a seed in one of those fruits, a member of one of their bodies, dependent for our fate, not on ourselves but on the fruit in which we belong.[85]

The first Adam represents all of us in our natural state, beloved yet sinful. God "has put eternity into man's heart, yet so that he cannot find out what God has done from the beginning to the end" (Eccles. 3: 11). We yearn for God, but live separated from him by our mortal frailty and our depraved hearts. We long for freedom yet find ourselves bound for condemnation. We are unable to keep ourselves alive (Ps. 22: 29). But the last Adam, Christ Jesus, represents the new creation. He is humanity remade, and by the work of the Holy Spirit through faith, we can be relocated out of the old Adam and into the last Adam, man remade in Christ. This is not an automatic transfer but occurs through reception of what the next Adam has done. The potential remains for "justification and life for all men" (Rom. 5: 18) through the one act of righteousness (an act which includes his life, death and resurrection) of Jesus. Indeed, Paul declares sweepingly that "in Christ God was reconciling the world to himself" (2 Cor. 5: 19). Then in the very next verse, he urges his readers, "We implore you on behalf of Christ, be reconciled to

God." Paul's deep argument is that the events of Jesus, in which our humanity was reconciled to God in him, must be received by each person in faith in order for the transfer of headship to occur. The work of the *one* new Adam was on behalf of the *many* trapped in the old Adam. Yet, *each* of the many must appropriate by faith the work of the One. By faith, we are transferred from the old to the new Adam.

The Ultimate Recap

In the second century, Irenaeus, bishop in Lyon, thought through the implications of Paul's teaching. Irenaeus anchored his theology in the word Paul used in Ephesians 1: 10 in speaking of God's purpose in Christ, "to unite all things in him, things in heaven and things on earth." This Greek word translated as "unite" is from the verb *anakephalaioo*, the literal meaning of which is to "again head." This means Jesus sums up, or gathers, the scattered creation under his headship. He re-heads the human race. Irenaeus went even farther in asserting that Jesus "commenced afresh the long line of human beings."[86] In Christ, "God recapitulated in himself the ancient formation of man, that He might kill sin, deprive death of its power, and vivify man."[87] Jesus, then, is the restart of the human race. He passed through all the stages of human life, gathering up and recapping who we are and what we do, but this time in faithfulness and perfection, reworking our very humanity from within. So Irenaeus writes, "He had Himself, therefore, flesh and blood, recapitulating in Himself not a certain other, but that original handiwork of the Father, seeking out that thing which had perished."[88]

For Irenaeus, it was very important that Christ the new Adam, the beginning and head of a new humanity, retrieved and saved the old Adam, the literal first man. His theology takes us back to the time in Jesus' journey between his cross and resurrection when he made his victory and new life known to the dead who awaited him. He writes,

> For the Lord, having been born "the First-begotten of the dead," and receiving into His bosom the ancient fathers, has regenerated them into the life of God, He having been made Himself the beginning of those that live, as Adam became the beginning of those who die. Wherefore also Luke, commencing the genealogy with the Lord, carried it back to Adam, indicating that it was He who regenerated them into the Gospel of life, and not they Him.

> It was necessary, therefore, that the Lord, coming to the lost sheep, and making recapitulation of so comprehensive a dispensation, and seeking after His own handiwork, should save *that very man* who had been created after His image and likeness, that is, Adam. . . . For if man, who had been created by God that he might live, after losing life, through being injured by the serpent that had corrupted him, should not any more return to life, but should be utterly and forever abandoned to death, God would in that case have been conquered. . . . [But], by means of the second man did He bind the strong man, and spoiled his goods, and abolished death, vivifying that man who had been in a state of death. . . . When therefore the Lord vivifies man, that is, Adam, death is at the same time destroyed. . . . But inasmuch as man is saved, it is fitting that he [Adam] who was created the original man should be saved.[89]

Jesus in atoning for sin and defeating both death and the devil redeemed Adam, both as the particular man and as the representative of our humanity. He recreated human nature free from sin and the deathly consequences of sin. But it is necessary for the particular man Adam to be relocated into the new Adam.

That's where the truth lies in the icon of the raising of Adam. The picture is not meant to be a photographic representation of the moment, but a rendering of the spiritual truth in the actual event that is beyond our sight. Jesus grabbed Adam by the hand and raised him to life. The recreation of our humanity in Jesus opens a possibility for all Adamic humanity which nevertheless has to be individually applied. We do not get recreated in ourselves, but only in union with Christ. So Irenaeus would maintain the interplay between the one and the many, the universal and the particular by saying, "For He came to save all through means of Himself— all, I say, who through Him are born again to God."[90]

A fourth century sermon captures the heart of the event of raising Adam. In considering what Jesus did in spirit while his body slept in the tomb, the preacher declares,

> He has gone to search for Adam, our first father, as for a lost sheep. Greatly desiring to visit those who live in darkness and in the shadow of death, he has gone to free from sorrow Adam in his bonds and Eve, captive with him - He who is both their God and the son of Eve. . . . "I am your God, who for your sake have become your son. . . . I order you, O sleeper, to awake. I did not create you to be a prisoner in hell. Rise from the dead, for I am the life of the dead."[91]

What an extraordinary affirmation: *I did not create you to be a prisoner in hell.* Jesus restored us to our creational purpose. He went all the way back to the root of humanity. He started his reclamation with the first man, and then extended it through all who were awaiting him. This is the event that came to be known as the Harrowing of Hell.

From the beginning the church has affirmed that Jesus' salvation worked "backward" in time as well as it does forward. All of those who would believe, whether before or after Jesus' historical life, were included in his mighty acts of redemption. While we might well eschew the mythological motifs that accrued through the centuries, we can still recognize that Sunday before sunrise was the event-basis for a salvation that extended to people both past and future. Adam was a representative man. After all, his name is based on the word for dust, and is used hundreds of times to mean generic mankind. But his name is also used in Scripture about a specific person. He was a particular man, and Jesus raised him from Sheol into life.

Commenting on the icon of the raising of Adam, the Eastern Orthodox theologians Leonid Ouspensky and Vladimir Lossky articulate the relationship between the particular salvation of a man and the redeeming of human nature as such:

> By freeing the old Adam, and with him the whole of mankind from slavery to him who is the incarnation of sin, darkness and death, He laid the foundation of a new life for those who have united with Christ into a new reborn mankind. Thus the spiritual raising of Adam is represented in the icon of the Descent into Hell as a symbol of the coming resurrection of the body, the first-fruit of which was the Resurrection of Christ.[92]

Freeing the man Adam, the root of our race, all humanity gained, in potential, freedom from slavery to sin. The devil's power was broken. But this new life and freedom come into being in each particular person only as he or she by the Spirit through faith is united to Christ.

Doxological Treasure:
The Hands Which Made Me

So far we have attempted to apprehend both the actuality of Adam and the resurrection of Jesus in the same body in which he was crucified.[93] We have admitted the limits of our sight into the realm beyond us and thereby constrained ourselves to what we can know from Scripture, both through specific passages and in its overall trajectory. With such understanding, we need no longer be concerned that exercises in holy imagination through the centuries need to be construed as literal events. Rather, able to discern what is speculative from what is known to be actual, we become free to be moved, and even informed, by some of the great works of imaginative theology.

In a 4th century section of the Latin edition of *The Gospel of Nicodemus*, we read of the encounter between the rising Jesus and the Adam long imprisoned in Sheol. Again, granting the truth of the event that Jesus encountered Adam, we may yet recognize that this is not a news report. What follows explores the meaning within such a moment. We will hear the relief, the tearful joy, of Adam and Eve learning that the ruin they brought upon the world was at last restored in Christ. They rejoice as he comes to reclaim them on the way to his resurrection.

> And behold, suddenly Hades trembled, and the gates of death and the bolts were shattered, and the iron bars were broken and fell to the ground, and everything was laid open.

> Then the Lord Jesus, the Savior of all, affectionate and most mildly saluting Adam kindly, said to him: "Peace be to you Adam, with your children, through immeasurable ages to ages!" Amen.

Then father Adam, falling forward at the feet of the Lord, and being raised erect, kissed his hands, and shed many tears, saying, testifying to all: Behold the hands which fashioned me!"

And he said to the Lord, "You have come, O King of glory, delivering men, and bringing them into Your everlasting Kingdom."

Then also our mother Eve in like manner fell forward at the feet of the Lord, and was raised erect, and kissed His hands, and poured forth tears in abundance, and said, testifying to all: "Behold the hands which made me!"[94]

Consider the immeasurable relief in Adam's words, "Behold the hands which fashioned me!" He might well have said, "Oh, you came for us! You came, you came, you came! I have not seen those hands since we walked in the Garden together. I have been cut off for centuries from the God who made me. Now at last you have appeared. You remembered. You did not leave us to languish in the shadows forever. You saved us!" What had been lost was restored. The millennia old curse was lifted. The ancient grief was assuaged. The Triune God did not forget. He came for Adam as the first act of the incarnate Son's rising from death. He who retains a human form into eternity, the last Adam, clasped the hand of the first Adam. By his Creator hand, he who is Man-made-new then made Adam anew. So he opened his recreating work to all who will entrust themselves to him. *Jesus descended fully into our death in order to raise us fully into his life.*

DESCENDING TO THE WORLD'S HELL: WHY THE DESCENT MATTERS TODAY

T he raising of the spirit of Adam from the prison of Sheol was a foundational event in Jesus' journey to raise all his people into resurrection life. In this chapter, we want to consider how, by his Spirit, Jesus continues to descend to the hell of lives that are by nature separated from God, retrieving us from a world hostile to God, and thereby transferring our inborn status as children of wrath to that of beloved children and heirs. We will look first at three states of spiritual deprivation which Jesus fills.

1) From All This Soul-Emptiness

In the events from cross to resurrection, Jesus opened up the prison of Sheol. Jesus traversed the lost lands of the realm that follows dying. Jesus hazarded this sojourn in order to blaze a road to life in the trackless desert. He plumbed the inky abyss of separation from God in order to shine in the place where once no light could penetrate. Jesus made hell unnecessary and no longer inevitable. Now he is the experienced guide as he takes us into everlasting life. The spiritual dynamic of Jesus' once-for-all descent and resurrection is repeated in every act of regeneration. Every time someone comes to Christ it is because Jesus, by his Spirit, has descended into his heart. This is his journey into our personal hells, in which he makes "of this abyss a road."[95]

In the fourth century, Macarius, one of the Egyptian desert fathers, preached about the relationship between the events of Jesus' descent to hell to free Adam and the spiritual rebirth that occurs in each soul united to Jesus. Macarius admits that the narrative of Jesus' descent seems foreign to our daily lives. But then he reminds his congregation that each heart is a tomb. Each soul is dead and therefore every person is the very terrain of death. Each person in Adam is bound and captive. Macarius' connections are beautiful:

> But when you hear that at that time the Lord delivered the souls from hell and darkness, and went down to hell, and did a glorious work, do not imagine that these things are so very far from your own soul. Man is capable of admitting and receiving the evil one. Death keeps fast hold of the soul of Adam, and the thoughts of the soul lie imprisoned in the darkness. When you hear of [tombs], do not think only of visible ones; your own heart is . . . a tomb.

> Well, then, the Lord comes into souls that seek after Him, into the deep of the heart-hell, and there lays His command upon death, saying, "Bring out the imprisoned souls that are seeking after Me, which thou detainest by force." So He breaks through the heavy stones that lie on the soul, opens the [tombs], raises up the man that is dead indeed, brings out of the dark jail the imprisoned soul.[96]

Since Pentecost, Jesus who descended into Sheol once-for-all as an event in the work of our redemption, descends by his Spirit again and again into the hell of souls separated from the Triune God.

Christ's great transit of mercy continues through the work of the Holy Spirit. He goes to the "heart-hell" of our spiritually dead, condemned and enchained souls in order to bring new life. Christ enters the petrified soul that has forsaken God. He plants in us seed from the Tree of Life that we might grow green unto God again. Macarius discerns both the objective journey of Jesus' work and the subjective journey of Christ to each heart:

> In His own person He enters into two quarters, into the depth of hell, and into the deep gulf of the heart, where the soul with its thoughts is held fast by death, and brings up out of the darksome hole the Adam that lay dead.[97]

Macarius sees clearly the connection between the event of Jesus' sojourn in hellish Sheol and his continual descent as heart by heart he enters those he saves. Christ has to restore even my ruined capacity to choose him.[98] He has to restore my will in order for my will freely to trust him.

Christ once entombed came by his Spirit to the tomb of my estranged life. He, who braved the stench of four-days-dead Lazarus, inhaled the rancid fumes of my rotting soul as he reached into my depths with his new life. Jesus did not turn from identifying with the full horror of the consequences of human sin. So now the triumphant savior does not eschew reaching his holy hands into my sticky guilt. He penetrates the venom sack in my soul and washes it clean with his Spirit. No hell of heart is too stained, too hot, too hard or too remote for the God who went beyond the ends of the universe of human experience to save us.

Paul wrote, "For God, who said, 'Let light shine out of darkness,' has shone in our hearts to give the light of the knowledge of the glory of God in the face of Jesus Christ" (2 Cor. 4: 6). The Triune God created all that is *ex nihilo*. He made something out of nothing. The act of saving a lost sinner is akin to creation. We require an act of God equivalent in quality to creating all things out of nothing. Moreover, we were beyond the neutrality of nothingness. We were in hostile estrangement from God. In descending into the hellish state of God-forsakenness and being raised from it, Jesus blazed the path of our salvation. He established the pattern of transference from the domain of darkness to the kingdom of God's beloved Son (Col. 1: 13). Along that way of his descent and ascent, Jesus now, through his Spirit, goes down into the sentence of condemnation, the lethal estrangement and the spiritual deathliness that is a human being without him. Conferring upon us reclaimed sinners his forgiveness and the power of his endless life (Heb. 7: 16), Christ then brings us up into light and life once more. Having gone further away from the Father than we can fall, and ascending higher to the throne than we can reach, the history of Jesus the representative man encompasses his people within the sheltering embrace of his journey on our behalf. Jesus' descent into hell reminds us that no one is beyond his reach. Anyone who yet breathes in this world, no matter how seemingly hopeless or soiled, can yet be retrieved should Christ come down by his Spirit and then the lost by faith consent to be taken up with him.

2) From All This Lonely Dying

The descent of Jesus resolves the profound loneliness we experience now and the greater loneliness we fear in death. In our heart of hearts, we worry that no one truly knows us. We make our way, even among our closest companions, as strangers. We also anticipate that we are each all alone at the last. So we anxiously await the death which removes us from the world and all we love. Even if we know that our relationships of "love" never really penetrated the isolation of our souls, they are yet all we have. We do not want to lose them. But no one can prevent our bodily dissolution. We fear death, as we think in our earthly end we will sink alone into either oblivion or an afterlife that might be far worse than this lonely, difficult world.

As a younger theologian, Joseph Ratzinger (Benedict XVI) engaged this experience of loneliness that afflicts the contemporary world. He addressed the existentialism which has been gripping Western culture ever tighter since Nietzsche. Modern humanity's bold assertion that we are on our own, with no god above to constrict us, also led to the sickening realization that we are thus profoundly *alone* in the cosmos. There is no one to guide us but ourselves. After the heady feeling that I create my own meaning comes the despair that I cannot sustain in myself any reason to live. All is futile. All is lonely. All leads to death. Rather than deny outright the despairing conclusions of existentialism, however, Ratzinger asserted that Christ has undergone these extremes precisely so that we do not have to be alone.

Ratzinger acknowledges that the existentialists have unmasked "the abyss of loneliness of man in general, who is alone in his innermost being." Even though this loneliness is "usually thickly overlaid" with our work and interactions, it is "nevertheless the true situation of man." This reality makes us at odds with our deepest needs, for we cannot exist alone. We yearn for companionship.[99]

Jesus experienced the stripping of all that masks, and thereby makes tolerable, our deep loneliness. The overlays of friendship and family, of having an accepted place in society, of counting on the rule of just law, of busy work and participation in worship were all taken from him in the Passion. He was abandoned on every front. No comforting hand reached him in that dark. No reassuring word broke the silence. No spiritual peace softened the rejection. Ratzinger describes,

> If there were such a thing as a loneliness that could no longer be penetrated and transformed by the word of another; if a state of abandonment were to arise that was so deep that no "You" could reach into it

anymore, then we should have real, total loneliness and dreadfulness, what theology calls "hell." It denotes a loneliness that the word love can no longer penetrate and that therefore indicates the exposed nature of existence in itself. Thus hell, despair, would dwell at the very bottom of our existence, in the shape of that loneliness which is as inescapable as it is dreadful. Death is absolute loneliness. But the loneliness into which love can no longer advance is—hell.[100]

That is what Jesus underwent in his sojourn in the realm of Sheol. Having been abandoned on the cross, he experienced an aloneness so total that he was a soul without even a microscopic scrap of love. Yes, he still existed, which in itself is some evidence of life and therefore of a Creator and therefore of a relationship, but his every awareness in Sheol spoke not of connection but rejection. He knew the despair of utter failure; the end of which is only aloneness.

That, paradoxically, is why *our* existential loneliness may be assuaged. For now we cannot go where Jesus has not gone. We cannot die more forsaken than he did. We cannot fall into a deeper hell than he experienced. Ratzinger writes,

> Christ strode through the gate of our final loneliness . . . in his Passion he went down into the abyss of our abandonment. Where no voice can reach us any longer, there is he. Hell is thereby overcome, or, to be more accurate, death, which was previously hell, is hell no longer. Neither is the same any longer because there is life in the midst of death, because love dwells in it. Now only deliberate self-enclosure is hell, or, as the Bible calls it, the second death.[101]

Death's grip is broken. Christ has shattered the cell doors of Hades. We don't have to stay in the lonely, personal hell of our sin. We don't have to fear everlasting separation from our Lord or our loved ones. The entire experience of death is different for those in Christ. Amidst the tears common to all at graveside, a quiet peace pervades those who know the one who harrowed hell.

In discovering the depths of Jesus' great transit of mercy, hope arises even for those who have lost loved ones to suicide. Some we love seem to be undergoing a despair untouchable by all our psychiatric skill. But Jesus who descended to hell is not baffled by their experience. Some we love experience an internal contradiction so strong it seems only self-violence can resolve it. But Jesus, caught in the crossfire of human rejection and divine wrath upon the cross, has already resolved every source of shame and every situation of paradox in his own divine/human person. His active work of offering himself into the helplessness of crucifixion becomes the resolution of even the deepest conflicts we feel. Whereas our self-harm will *not* soothe the pain, pay the price incurred, or fill the voids we undergo, Christ's self-offering has created an atonement that dissolves even seemingly indelible stains.

Some in pain step out of bounds, off the playing field of our attempts to love them. We are dismayed, but Jesus himself went off the map into the wasteland of hell. There are no regions of human experience unknown to him. The Father did not rescue his Son immediately from the cross. He underwent the plummet into Holy Saturday so that we cannot leap, no matter how angrily we push off, beyond his embrace of all human suffering. He knows. And still he loves. We have not the power to negate that love even by the rashest act. We are not alone, nor are the most tangled and wayward wandering of his sheep. We enfold them into Christ's care. So Catherine Aslanoff triumphantly declares, "Christ's descent into hell is his presence in our various hells, both personal and collective; our illnesses, our infirmities, our wars, our gulags, our asylums, our murders, our suicides, our death."[102]

3) Through All The Sorrow of Life

We innately move away from whatever creates discomfort. The body protects itself from injury through pain, so that we naturally avoid what hurts us. We turn as well from emotional pain. Who would willingly welcome stinging tears of grief or the sick feeling in the pit of the stomach that betrayal brings? Yet Jesus in his arc of descending turns from none of these.

The events of Jesus' descent through the cross into death are transformative for our experience of suffering. He passed through the most difficult human emotions all the while processing them honestly in raw faithfulness before his Father. Whatever we undergo, Jesus has known the depths of it in his descent. This goes beyond the comfort of empathy. Joined to him by the Spirit, we have *communion* with Christ in our suffering. He takes up even our despair in his intercessions before his Father's throne. But he does so because he has already "borne our griefs and carried our sorrows" (Isa. 53: 4) in his redemptive work. He maintains a steady connection to them even now. Jesus ministers to us out of his own experience of suffering.

But more, we can discover how our suffering enables us to participate in the suffering of Christ. Not that Jesus needs to suffer any more in order to have atoned for our sins. Of course not. But Paul had a mystical awareness that his sufferings were "filling up what is lacking in Christ's afflictions" (Col. 1: 24). Paul certainly found no want of sufficiency in Christ's suffering to redeem us from sin. But he knew that when we offer up our pain and sorrow to Jesus, we may make a connection with the events of his suffering. They remain a vivid part of his experience and therefore a touchpoint with us. So, we offer our pain and realize that what we undergo actually enables us to identify with Jesus. We know some little bit of what he underwent for us. Jesus identified with stark human experience more directly and deeply than any one of us ever will.

When we suffer, we find points of contact with events of his life and find ourselves closer to him.

Jesus' descent into forsakenness led to glorious resurrection and will eventually result in the making new of all things (Rev. 21: 5). Our lives will follow a similar pattern. Our willing embrace of the suffering we cannot avoid anyway can lead to spiritual renewal. The history of Jesus frees us to enter the inevitable sorrow of life with both confidence and hope. [103]

We can be *realists*. We can accept the sorrow interlaced with all our days as taken up in the life of God-with-us. This is the way it is. It's not the way it was intended. But suffering will endure until Christ returns to set all things right. In this interim time, we know by our union with Jesus in every stage of his journey, that even the hardest sorrows will be transformed to means of redemption and occasions for praise.

One dear to me has battled to find hope in the midst of depression. All hinges on the ability of Jesus to go under what crushed her and lift her up. All depends on his history of receiving sorrow at its root, taking it all upon himself as the man of tears and rising in joy that does not dismiss, but accounts for and redeems, what makes us so sad. One day, as she prayed, she visualized the risen Jesus with her. Without trying, she heard him speak. Gently, briefly, he addressed her. "I understand. My hope runs deeper than your sadness." In that moment, she knew in her bones that she was not alone. All this dying, all this leaving, all this loneliness was rising in new life. *My hope runs deeper than your sadness.*

These words only have realistic meaning if they are grounded in events that truly happened. Jesus sojourned through the despair of unredeemed humanity so that by arising he could truly affirm that his hope, which endured beyond hope in the place of no hope, runs deeper than all our sadness. By this hope, we can affirm the words Frances Spufford imagined Jesus speaking on Easter to his startled disciples. "Don't be afraid, says Yeshua. Far more can be mended than you know."[104] Indeed.

Another Chance?

As we move toward conclusion, one final, enduring question awaits. What does Jesus' descent have to do with the salvation of those who lived before the incarnation, those who have never heard of Jesus and/or those who, having heard the gospel did not receive it in this lifetime? The church has always affirmed that the people of God who lived before Jesus came would be saved by Jesus through their faith in the LORD and his promises. They departed the world into Sheol like all humankind. But their lives were marked by trust in the LORD I AM as the redeemer of his people. Some had informed faith, such as Abraham who offered Isaac believing that "God was able even to raise him from the dead" (Heb. 11: 19). Moses trusted that "The LORD your God will raise up for you a prophet like me" (Deut. 18: 15). Job proclaimed even amidst intense suffering, "For I know that my Redeemer lives, and at the last he will stand upon the earth" (Job 19: 25). But most of the believers in ancient Israel could never have imagined how God would save them. Paul affirms that the full revelation of the incarnation of the Son of God in Jesus, a surprising mystery, "was not made known to the sons of men in other generations as it has now been revealed" (Eph. 3: 5). So Jesus, encountering their spirits in Sheol, had to make himself known as savior. He had to reveal his identity to them. These souls were illumined and their faith transformed from varying levels of ignorance into knowledge. Such recognition of the savior by those spirits in Sheol indicates a salvific fulfillment beyond what they could have experienced in this world. As Hebrews 11: 13 says, "These all died in faith, not having received the things promised, but having seen them and greeted them from afar, and having acknowledged that they were strangers and exiles on the earth." So Jesus raised from Sheol the spirits of all those who had been awaiting a savior, albeit with inchoate faith.

But if it was possible for the departed spirits of people of the covenant to grow, after death, in their knowledge and acceptance of Jesus as savior, might it be possible for others to do the same? For instance, we might consider those yet to be born who would die without ever knowing the gospel. We wonder what happens to those who have never heard of Jesus. Will they have opportunity to make a decision for Christ when they see him face to face? Is it only a matter of election, by which ignorance will be no excuse? Or does election mean that some who lived here with no knowledge of Jesus will receive and be enabled to believe in Christ as savior? Will any, some, or all get to encounter Jesus face to face with the possibility of being united to him by faith? In other words, will everyone get a "first" chance?

This line of questions of course raises another. We also wonder about those who heard misshapen news about Jesus. They rejected a gospel that was not the gospel, and the distortions were so strong they never could grasp the true good news. It seems both compassionate and reasonable that those who associated the name of Christ with a hater or a hitter, will have a chance after death to see the name of Christ associated with the savior who loves them, and thereby respond. But are there sufficient grounds for such hope?[105]

The possibility after death of a first, clear encounter that can lead to salvation has also raised questions about *second* opportunities. Perhaps we might, when driven to our knees by the glory radiating from Christ's "rich wounds yet visible above in beauty glorified"[106] cry out a confession like that of Thomas, "My Lord and my God!" (John 20: 28). At that late hour, would that profession and submission be enough? The heart yearns for it to be so. Especially in the case of our loved ones, we want to plead, "Isn't that what you wanted all along? The cry for mercy? The recognition of who you are? The bowing of the knee?" But there is for us making such inquiry a stark realization that down that road glaring signs rear up which say, "No trespassing!" Jesus' own words block that path. He speaks of the Day of Judgment as a master who "has risen and shut the door." Many will knock at the door and cry out "Lord, open to us." But the master will answer, "I do not know where you come from." There will be "weeping and gnashing of teeth" for those who find themselves cast out (Luke 13: 22-30).[107] The urgency to take the first opportunity shoots through the Scriptures.

Though C. S. Lewis' generous views on encountering Christ after death go beyond the limits of my confessional tradition, his insights in this brief letter cut straight to the heart of the issue:

> . . . the doctrine of Christ's descending into Hell and preaching to the dead: that would be outside time, and include those who died before He was born as Man. I don't think we know the details: we must just stick to the view that (a) All justice & mercy will be done, (b) But that nevertheless it is our duty to do all we can to convert unbelievers.[108]

All justice and mercy will be done. That gives me hope that everyone will be given at least a first, clear chance to respond to the gospel, either in this life or the next. This is my hope and it appears to be founded on the trajectory of Jesus' history from Scripture. It makes theological sense. And yet, there is no explicit teaching of a first chance *post mortem*, let alone a second chance. With Lewis, I trust God fully to be both just and merciful. But hope is not doctrine and so this position cannot be proclaimed as definite from pulpit or seminary lectern. This is a hope, perhaps a well-founded hope, but not a certainty.[109] Therefore there remains the urgency that the time is now for the gospel to be proclaimed and believed. There is no salvation outside of Jesus Christ, and this moment may be all that any of us has.

One of the reasons for hesitation in affirming Jesus' descent to the dead and his interaction with those in Sheol is that it may become associated with this speculation of "post-mortem evangelism." Moreover, this episode of Jesus' history raises questions of the medieval descriptions of a limbo for the church fathers and a purgatory for the rest of us. But by this point we have seen that these questions are peripheral to the meaning of Jesus' descent for us.[110] Those queries ask for knowledge beyond the sight given to us. I had hoped that my research into the descent would lead me to express confidently this wider hope for all to hear and, eventually, for all to believe. I still hope so. But I do not *know* so. I may not affirm so. Scripture and my own Reformed confessions do not open that road.

What we can say to all who will hear is that in a world of sorrow, Christ has taken up all our suffering and embraced it unto deepest death. In his rising, he has redeemed even the worst that we can undergo. He exchanges with us now his forgiveness for our guilt, his peace for our fear, his love for our estrangement and his everlasting life to renew all our dying. I can describe a magnificent salvation accomplished in the sojourn of Jesus through hell and death. The application of that redemption in the next life cannot confidently be offered beyond the conditions of Scripture. But in regards to our inclusion, I can with certainty only say, "Receive it *now*." More poetically, George Herbert issued this Easter invitation, made first to his own soul:

> Arise sad heart. If thou dost not withstand,
>   Christ's resurrection thine may be:
> Do not by hanging down break from the hand,
>   Which as it riseth, raiseth thee.[111]

Sent to the World's Hell

Jesus descended into our death in order to raise us up fully into his life. His great Paschal voyage directs the mission of his church. The way to participate in his redeeming passage is for us to descend into the world's brokenness with the love of Christ.

We are to follow the lines of his great transit of mercy toward the world. That is the only way to experience vibrantly the spiritual ascension of being joined to his rising. Paradoxically, the way up to Jesus now ascended follows the way down to the least and the lost. Benedict once concluded his Easter vigil homily with a prayer which links the church in mission to the descending and ascending of Christ:

> Lord, show us that love is stronger than hatred, that love is stronger than death. Descend into the darkness and the abyss of our modern age, and take by the hand those who await you. Bring them to the light! In my own dark nights, be with me to bring me forth! Help me, help all of us, to descend with you into the darkness of all those people who are still waiting for you, who out of the depths cry unto you! Help us to bring them your light! Help us to say the "yes" of love, the love that makes us descend with you and, in so doing, also to rise with you. Amen![112]

Jesus' descent into hell to raise Adam is the pattern for the mission of Christ's church. We go to the worst places with the greatest news. We go to the discarded with embracing arms of welcome. We go to the deepest darkness so that the light of Christ might shine the brightest. The specific places and circumstances to which we are sent are as unique as each congregation and every believer. But the field of our service is not less than humankind in its state of bondage to decay (Rom. 8: 21) and sin, resulting in oppression and misery.

Scottish theologian William Milligan reminds the church that she is "the representative of the dying, living Lord." Therefore, ". . . there is no want or human weakness strange to her. It is her part to heal every wound and wipe away every tear."[113] The world wilts under the perception that these present days are but the emptiness and hopelessness of Holy Saturday. The powers arrayed against our flourishing seem to have triumphed. The dream of hope has dissipated and the cynic in a thousand ways quips that the defeated silence of Saturday is all we should expect. But the church knows better. The day of darkness has gestated the new creation. We have a gospel to proclaim which accounts now for all this suffering, dying and loneliness with authentic hope. Our hopeful work is everywhere to everyone.

Eucatastrophe

Finally, we want to relate Jesus' descent to our hope for the ultimate renewal of the world. J.R.R. Tolkien reflected only briefly in print on the function of stories such as his trilogy, *The Lord of the Rings*. But his comments take us straight to the narrative of a descending savior who entered defeat in order to gain victory. Tolkien coined the phrase *eucatastrophe* to express the sudden reversal in a story that leads to a longed for, but unexpected happy ending. This is the resolution against all odds that stirs hope in the human heart that the world's destiny will not be the death and destruction toward which it appears to rush. Tolkien wrote in a letter to his son that the eucatastrophe in a story:

> ... pierces you with a joy that brings tears ... it produces its peculiar effect because it is a sudden glimpse of Truth, your whole nature . . . feels a sudden relief as if a major limb out of joint had suddenly snapped back. It perceives . . . that this is indeed how things really do work in the Great World for which our souls were made . . . the Resurrection was the greatest eucatastrophe possible . . . and produces that essential emotion: Christian joy which produces tears because it is qualitatively so like sorrow, because it comes from those places where Joy and Sorrow are at one, reconciled, as selfishness and altruism are lost in love.[114]

The more deadly the danger, the greater the near defeat and the more dire its consequences, the more elation eucatastrophic resolution creates. Tolkien explains that a truly glorious ending does not arise from an inevitable outcome of good. Concerning eucatastrophe, he writes,

> It does not deny the existence of dyscatastrophe, of sorrow and failure: the possibility of these is necessary to the joy of deliverance; it denies (in the face of much evidence, if you will) universal final defeat and in so far is *evangelium*, giving a fleeting glimpse of Joy, Joy beyond the walls of the world, poignant as grief.
>
> The Birth of Christ is the eucatastrophe of Man's history. The Resurrection is the eucatastrophe of the story of the Incarnation. The story begins and ends in joy.... There is no tale ever told that men would rather find was true ... [115]

Jesus' journey of descent into our death included his engagement with the powers of evil at every stage. Defeat was always possible. We miss the power of these gospel events if we look at Christ's victory as only and always inevitable. We sanitize away the glory if we think that God risked nothing by emptying himself to walk among us truly as a man. But the gospels take our breath away when we realize how ruin ever remained a word or step away. Faithfulness had to be chosen every moment by our savior. To realize the joy of gospel eucatastrophe, we have to consider the actual threats at every turn. The murderous intent from Herod against Jesus in infancy was real. In the wilderness, Jesus could have succumbed to the devil's temptations. Jesus' tears over Lazarus' death opened an opportunity to give in to the human despair of grief. Jesus could have walked away from the pressure in Gethsemane, refusing the cup. Going to the cross, Jesus hazarded universal defeat on behalf of the human race. He could have stayed dead.

Holy Saturday demands that we engage the potential ruin in the crucifixion before grasping too quickly for resolution. On Holy Saturday, the possibility of dyscatastrophe remained: that God could be forsaken by God; that the victorious Son could be conscious only of everlasting defeat; that his vision of death could keep him in an abyss of hopelessness. This defeat appeared to be final and must be felt that way, if we are to understand the wisdom and the wonder of the victory plan, hidden even from the angels, which the Triune God intended to enact all along.

All turned, beyond hope, on the clarion call of the Father. He summoned back his Son as he sent the reviving Spirit to awaken, reunite and transform the soul and body of the crucified God/Man. Jesus had gone beyond our farthest exile, dug beneath the fiercest thorn, fallen under the deepest ocean of separation. So he came back bearing it all, raising up all of creation with him. Now he is exalted above every name that is named and every knee "in heaven and on earth and under the earth" will bow to him (Phil. 2: 10).

The new creation begun in resurrection cannot be stopped. All the scattered threads are being gathered and resewn. Earth and heaven, flesh and spirit, sinful man and holy God have been reconciled (Col. 1: 20, 2 Cor. 5: 18). Joy, while yet leaving no tear unaccounted for, catches up and transforms all sorrow. Jesus was once the loneliest creature in existence, but from the moment of resurrection the day has been dawning which will reach its zenith at his mighty return. And Jesus will be seen to be the center of a teeming, intimate and glorious new humanity enfolded into the everlasting life of the Triune God, ruling with him over a restored creation.

At that midsummer, that shimmering noon, the thunderous, symphonic, Eucharistic song of creation will be led by the One who alone could conduct it. He will sing the psalm written for him so long ago, "Let the heavens be glad, and let the earth rejoice; let the sea roar, and all that fills it; let the field exult and everything in it!" (Ps. 96: 11-12). The trees of Eden at last raised from shadows

(Ez. 31: 16-18) will fulfill the vision of the psalm for all creation that day, "Then shall all the trees of the forest sing for joy before the LORD, for he comes, for he comes to judge the earth" (Ps. 96: 12-13). The eucatastrophe of Jesus' journey evokes mirth in triumphant tears of joy, tears of sorrow summoned, gathered and everlastingly redeemed.

Doxological Treasure

Now we give the last word to the man known as Golden-Mouth. In the 4th century, John Chrysostom, Archbishop of Constantinople, preached an Easter message that has been read in Orthodox churches every Easter since:

> Let no one fear death, for the Death of our Savior
> Has set us free.
> He has destroyed it by enduring it.
> He destroyed Hell when He descended into it.
> He put it into an uproar even as it tasted of His flesh.
>
> Isaiah foretold this when he said,
> "You, O Hell, have been troubled
> By encountering Him below."
> Hell was in an uproar because it was done away with.
> It was in an uproar because it is mocked.
> It was in an uproar, for it is destroyed.
> It is in an uproar, for it is annihilated.
> It is in an uproar, for it is now made captive.
>
> Hell took a body, and discovered God.
> It took earth, and encountered Heaven.
> It took what it saw, and was overcome by what it did not see.

O Death, where is thy sting?
O Hell, where is thy victory?

Christ is Risen, and you, O death, are annihilated!
Christ is Risen, and the evil ones are cast down!
Christ is Risen, and the angels rejoice!
Christ is Risen, and life is liberated!

Christ is Risen, and the tomb is emptied of its dead;
for Christ having risen from the dead,
is become the first-fruits of those who have fallen asleep.

To Him be Glory and Power forever and ever. Amen![116]

~ APPENDIX 1 ~

CLARIFYING THE TERMS

Technically, the subtitle of this book is wrong! Jesus did not descend into hell: if by hell we mean an infernal region governed by evil powers. Nor did he go to a divine grind house of punishment for sins where demons act as God's torturers, as if he needed to bear more wrath than on the cross.[117] Moreover, hell as a final state of eternal destruction, living death, for those who refuse the Lordship of Christ is yet to be created. That horrifying state will be a consequence of the return of the Judge in flesh to bring the world into alignment with his will. Jesus did not enter what will exist only in relationship to decisions about himself.[118]

So *hell* in any of those senses is not really what the church ever meant by the descent clause. One of the main sources of confusion about Christ's descent is that several words in the Hebrew and Greek Scriptures have all been translated as "hell" in many English Bibles (such as the King James Version). A single word translating multiple concepts muddies our understanding. We can clarify what actually is meant by Christ's descent into hell by looking closely at each term.

Sheol

In the Hebrew Scriptures, there was never thought that this life is all there is. But God had not yet revealed the glorious hope of our living in everlasting resurrection bodies in a renewed creation. For the people in Old Testament days, the shadowy realm of Sheol awaited those who died. Being in a realm beyond this one, Sheol is spoken of in a combination of both literal and metaphorical descriptions. Used more than 60 times, Sheol is always pictured as being *downward*. That directional orientation has made sense across all cultures and times. We are, after all, gravity-bound creatures. The vitality of life enables us to get up and work, worship, love and play. But age and illness steal our strength and eventually cause us to fall down (not up!) to death. Of course the ancient cosmologies differed from those we have today. But Scripture remarkably avoids being tied to a particular view of the universe. Plus, I don't really think the ancients thought you could spelunk down to Sheol if only you had a long enough rope and found the right opening. They understood that going down to Sheol meant the soul traveling further than the body to a place of departed spirits.

With this understanding that the inspired writers had more than the literal in mind, Sheol can be described as under the earth. So we read the graphic fate of Korah and those who rebelled against Moses: "the ground opens its mouth and swallows them up ... and they . . . go down alive into Sheol" (Num. 16: 30). Sheol can be under the bottom of the sea. So the sinking Jonah prayed, "I went down to the land whose bars closed upon me forever" (Jon. 2: 5-6). Sheol is also synonymous with the Pit (e.g., Jon. 2: 6, Ps. 30: 3, Isa. 14: 15). Imagining a landfill, we see the place of discard. Things tossed there do not get retrieved. When we enter the Pit of Sheol we are dismissed from relevance in the present land of the living to being forgotten in a realm from which we cannot escape.

Sheol appears to us as a ravenous power. In his struggle with Saul who almost killed him, David felt the grasping, entrapping grip of Sheol: "The cords of Sheol entangled me; the snares of death confronted me" (2 Sam. 22: 6, Ps. 18: 5). Sheol like a great dark mouth swallows the living (Prov. 1: 12), yet is always hungry for more people to consume (Prov. 27: 20, Hab. 2: 5).

In usual experience, no one returns from the dead. So Job declared, "As the cloud fades and vanishes, so he who goes down to Sheol does not come up" (Job 7: 9). In every ordinary life, Sheol means the place of no return, where we are not annihilated, but neither are we truly living.

In particular, David lamented that in Sheol the voices which praise God go silent. No more festival holy days full of music or boisterous feasts of remembrance. Yet, prophetically and perhaps well beyond his awareness, David expressed this dearth of worship in Sheol through questions. "For in death there is no remembrance of you; in Sheol who will give you praise?" (Ps. 6: 5). In Psalm 30 he lamented, "What profit is there in my death, if I go down to the pit? Will the dust praise you? Will it tell of your faithfulness?" Meant to be rhetorical, these questions seemingly could only be answered with a resounding "No!" The sons of Korah (could they be related to the same Korah swallowed by the earth?!) pick up this style in the darkest lament of the Bible, asking, "Do you work wonders for the dead? Do the departed rise up to praise you? Is your steadfast love declared in the grave? (Ps. 88: 10-11). Again, for centuries, worshipers could only shake their heads with a despondent negative. But expressing the diminishment of death as interrogatives left open the gloriously unexpected affirmative which the Son of God would make on Easter morning.

This hope is presaged in two lovely passages. Hannah, exulting that the LORD I AM had opened her womb to conceive Samuel, prayed, "The LORD kills and brings to life; he brings down to Sheol and raises up" (1 Sam. 1: 6). Many decades would pass, yet the LORD would prove right her praise, as through Elijah God raised the widow's son (1 Kings 17: 17-24), and then through Elisha raised two others (2 Kings 4: 34-35, 13: 21). All three of these who returned to life had to enter Sheol again. But the sons of Korah, again speaking beyond their present sight, foresaw a greater future: "But God will ransom my soul from the power of Sheol, for he will receive me" (Ps. 49: 15). Through such prayers, the hope endured that more life could follow lonely Sheol, a life to be lived in the intimate, immediate presence of God.

Conducting a detailed analysis of Scriptural texts, Reformed scholar Robert Morey succinctly summarizes the condition of those entering Sheol before death itself was transformed by the work of Jesus:

> At death man becomes a *rephaim*, i.e. a "ghost," "shade," or "disembodied spirit.". . . . Instead of describing man as passing into nonexistence, the Old Testament states that man becomes a disembodied spirit…Once in Sheol, all experiences related exclusively to physical life are no longer possible. Those in Sheol do not marry and procreate children because they do not have bodies. Neither do they plan and execute business transactions. Once in Sheol, they cannot attend public worship in the temple and give sacrifices or praise. There are no bodily pleasures such as eating and drinking. Those in Sheol do not have any wisdom or knowledge about what is happening in the land of the living. They are cut off from the living. They have entered a new dimension of reality with its own kind of existence. . . . And yet, those in Sheol have a form of consciousness. They 'converse with each other and even make moral judgement on the lifestyle of new arrivals (Is. 14: 19-20, Ez. 32: 21). They are thus conscious entities in Sheol.[119]

The Scripture passages referring to existence in Sheol are not as much didactic as analogical. They hint at the experience of the dead more than describe in precise detail what cannot ever be known on this side of death. For Sheol is a realm beyond human perception. With so little definite knowledge, we can certainly understand why Hebrews described humanity before Christ as "those who through fear of death were subject to lifelong slavery" (Heb. 2: 15). The next state did not, in the days before Jesus' resurrection, appear to be a good one.

Finally, we note that Sheol and the Pit were not only used to describe physical death. Scripture employs both terms to describe either deep sufferings of the soul, or situations of dire distress that could result in death but (obviously) did not. So, David gratefully rejoices, "For you have delivered my soul from the depths of Sheol" (Ps. 86: 13). And earlier, "you restored me to life from among those who go down to the pit" (Ps. 30: 3).

Hades

Used nine times in the New Testament, *Hades* is the Greek word which translates the Hebrew *Sheol*. So in Acts 2: 27, Peter quotes Psalm 16: 10 from the Greek Old Testament popular at the time. So we read, "For you will not abandon my soul to Hades." Thus Hades also means the realm of the souls of the dead.

Hades as the equivalent of Sheol is what Jesus had in mind in one of his encounters with the scribes and Pharisees. As if healing the blind, paralytic, and demon possessed, and even raising the dead were not enough, they asked Jesus for a miraculous sign to prove his authority for teaching. He declared that no further sign would be given than the sign of Jonah: "For just as Jonah was three days and three nights in the belly of the great fish, so will the Son of Man be three days and three nights in the heart of the earth" (Matt. 12: 40). This text is crucial for confirming that Jesus expected to be confined in the realm of the dead, his body in the tomb and his soul in Sheol/Hades, for the full time between cross and resurrection. Jesus, as he frequently did, spoke analogically. This text does not mean Jesus thought his soul would literally be in the magma of the earth. Nor does it mean that like Jonah he would have only a near-death experience. He expected a fully human death. It would have enough duration to be truly death. But it would not be forever. For, as we read elsewhere, Jesus also anticipated that on the third day he would rise (Matt. 16: 21, 17: 23, 20: 19).

Between the testaments, a greater hope had arisen for the resurrection of God's people at a great Day of Judgment.[120] Hades became considered an intermediate state where both the wicked and the righteous awaited this day. Jesus' parable of Lazarus and the rich man implies that there may be different regions of Hades.[121] There is a place of peace in Hades, Abraham's bosom (Luke 16: 22), sometimes called Paradise (Luke 23: 43), though it does not approach the bliss of heaven and the immediate presence of God. There is a place of torment in Hades (Luke 16: 23), though it does not approach the final outer darkness of the damned that we will read about in Revelation.

Hades and Death itself are also personified in the imagery of Revelation. Hades always follows Death, depicted as the rider on the pale horse in Rev. 6: 8. This makes sense, as Hades is the state to which the power of Death carries a person. Jesus, however, has mastered both powers, declaring, "I died, and behold I am alive forevermore, and I have the keys of Death and Hades" (Rev. 1: 18).

The same word, Hades, is used in Greek mythology for the underworld through which runs the River Styx, across which Charon ferries the dead souls. Conflating the two visions would be a problem for later theology. The New Testament, however, uses Hades not under the influence of Greek mythology but in consonance with Sheol.

Gehenna

Gehenna is the same word in both Hebrew and Greek designating the fiery place of everlasting punishment. Gehenna is a variation on Hinnom, a valley outside Jerusalem where children had been sacrificed in idolatrous rites (Jer. 7: 31, 32: 35). It later became a garbage dump, and its fires smoldered continually. By Jesus' time, the name of this notorious valley had become equated with punishment in the afterlife, a condition to occur after the intermediate state of Sheol and the Day of Judgment. Gehenna is what we usually think of as *hell*.

The New Testament records Gehenna spoken a dozen times from the lips of Jesus. He frightens us with warning, "And do not fear those who kill the body but cannot kill the soul. Rather fear him who can destroy both soul and body in hell [Gehenna]" (Matt. 10: 28). Lest we comfort ourselves that such words are merely for the reprobate, Jesus throws our theology into a tailspin by linking our failure in works of love with Gehenna. He said to his *disciples*, "But I say to you that everyone who is angry with his brother will be liable to judgment . . . whoever says, 'You fool!' will be liable to the hell (Gehenna) of fire" (Matt. 5: 22).

Hyperbolically, we hope, Jesus directs us to cut off a hand or tear out an eye should either cause us to sin. For these painful extremes would be far better than to be thrown into Gehenna for our sin (Mark 9: 42-49). Jesus uses the term Gehenna, then, as a kind of shorthand for what he describes elsewhere as the "eternal punishment" to which will be sent those who failed to do acts of kindness to "the least of these my brothers" (Matt. 25: 40, 45). It also encapsulates Jesus' teaching on the exaction of the Father against those who do not forgive their brother from the heart (Matt. 18: 35). Jesus did not hesitate to compare the burning sulphur that rained down on Sodom as more bearable than the cities which rejected him (Luke 10: 12). In this teaching, he actually uses the word Hades, though more in the sense of Gehenna, for it is the destructive destination of unbelieving Capernaum (Luke 10: 15).

Though he did not use the word, Gehenna is what Paul had in mind in speaking of the future of those who "do not obey the gospel of our Lord Jesus. They will suffer the punishment of eternal destruction, away from the presence of the Lord . . . when he comes on that day" (2 Thess. 1: 8-10). Revelation envisions Gehenna via "the lake that burns with fire and sulfur, which is the second death" (Rev. 21: 8). This is the portion given not only to the devil (Rev. 20:

10), but to "the cowardly, the faithless, the detestable . . . murderers, the sexually immoral, sorcerers, idolaters, and all liars" (Rev. 21: 8).

Relatedly, *tartarus* is a Greek concept of a place beneath Hades for the wicked. It is imported only once into the New Testament in reference to a prison in which fallen angels are kept before the Judgment Day (2 Pet. 2: 4, but alluded to in Jude 6).

Much as I might like, I find myself unable to relegate these passages about Sheol, Hades and Gehenna to a discard pile reserved for descriptions of primitive views of the afterlife. A close reading reveals that the Bible declines to get entangled in prevailing cosmologies. People then may have had an understanding of a three-storied universe with heaven above, hell below, and the earth in the center. But Scripture does not get committed to a Ptolemaic cosmos. Again, I am forced to take the texts on their own terms. The imagery they offer for existence after death is not fanciful. But neither is it limited to its literal interpretation. The vivid imagery directs us to realities beyond description, more horrible not less, than what is directly depicted. They make urgent our need for a redeemer who can free us from such an abysmal destiny.

Many Concepts, One Word

In spite of such distinction in the terms, for years, English Bibles confusingly translated *all* of these words as hell! Sheol, Hades, Tartarus and Gehenna were all rendered by the English *hell,* thus conflating the concepts in our minds. And now to confuse things even more, the clause in the Apostles' Creed *does not employ any of these root words!* When we read that Jesus "descended into hell," the ancient Latin and Greek versions are actually using *none* of the terms we discussed above. The Latin version says that Jesus descended *ad inferna,* or *inferos,* a term which means "underneath." Inferna thus means the underworld. The Greek version is based on *katotera* from Ephesians 4: 9, the lower regions of the earth, the netherworld. In the cosmology of the time, across the ancient world, the realm of the dead was considered to be below the earth. Departed spirits went down below. So to speak the creed with its original meaning, we really should follow the updated versions which declare, "He descended to the *dead*." That is to say, we affirm that after dying, Jesus entered the state, or realm, of death. Between the cross and resurrection Jesus became one of "the dead ones." His body lay in the tomb. His soul entered Sheol/Hades. The quality of such a sojourn in the realm of the dead, however, remains for exploration. As chapter 5 suggests, Sheol may well have been "hellish" for Jesus.

~ APPENDIX 2 ~

THE THIEF ON THE CROSS

One of the most beautiful conversations in the gospels occurs on the cross. In Luke 23, we read of the two criminals crucified on either side of Jesus. One said, "Jesus, remember me when you come into your kingdom." And Jesus replied to him, "Truly, I say to you, today you will be with me in Paradise" (Luke 23: 42-43). This magnificent promise gathers in a lost sheep in the final hours of life. At first glance, however, this passage seems problematic to an understanding that Jesus entered the realm of the dead after his crucifixion. For Jesus' words seem to imply that both the spirit of Jesus and that of the thief would on Good Friday be in heaven. How do we hold the joy of this affirmation together with Jesus' sojourn among the dead on Holy Saturday?

Briefly, here are five replies to consider in balancing the promise to the thief with other New Testament texts:

a) An interpretation that Jesus and the thief would be in heaven Friday afternoon would contradict Jesus' own prediction in Matthew 12: 40 that he would be three days and nights in the heart of the earth. While giving the promise to the thief its full due, we may not simply let it negate Jesus' own considered prediction. Jesus expected a sojourn among the dead. The texts remain in tension and need to be allowed to help interpret one another. Some alternatives to an immediate entry together into heaven include the following.

b) By Jesus' time, Jewish belief had begun to conjecture

different regions of the underworld. Some considered Paradise to be not in heaven, but part of Sheol where the righteous dead were in repose, awaiting the general resurrection. We see hints of this worldview in Jesus' parable about the rich man and Lazarus (Luke 16: 19-31). This place of rest was also known as Abraham's bosom (Luke 16: 22). That could be the Paradise Jesus meant here, though other New Testament references to Paradise (2 Cor. 12: 3, Rev. 2: 7) imply a more heavenly destination.

c) Ancient commentators noted that Paradise is wherever Jesus is, be it in the underworld or in heaven. To be reconciled to Jesus is to pass from death to life, from hell to paradise, even if one is hanging on a cross! The point of Jesus' words was that the thief would continue to be with him rather than enter condemnation after death.[122]

d) The commas were not originally in the Greek manuscripts. The text could be read, "I say to you today, you will be with me . . ." I used to think moving the comma was merely sleight of hand, especially as this is the record of a conversation, not a proclamation. (Compare Acts 20: 26 in which Paul says, "I testify to you this day that . . ."). But the context is important. The thief's request revealed that he believed Jesus was the Messiah who would usher in the "Day" of the LORD's active reign on earth. Jews of the time expected the LORD to come to the earth, drawing history to a halt and ushering in the age of the Kingdom of God. So the thief begged Jesus to remember him in that triumphant future. He didn't want to be forgotten when this conversation in shared agony would seem far distant in the glow of the King's reign. The thief's worldview anticipated that Jesus would pass through death into life, then return in glory to reign as king of heaven and earth. Jesus' reply was to give him assurance in that very moment, not in some future recollection, that the man would be with him in glory. He did not need to wait for the Day of the LORD to know he would be part of the Messiah's triumph. That time, paradoxically, was now, even though the passage through Saturday had not occurred.[123]

e) Building on the above, the "today" in this passage could be considered eschatologically. When Jesus completed his passion, the future Kingdom of God became present reality. A new age dawned after atonement was made and death's power broken. Even if Jesus still had to endure Sheol as a diminishment until Sunday, his sacrifice had been made, resurrection was inevitable and the "today" of God's new creation had begun. Joined to Jesus by faith, the thief would participate in that reality.[124]

Understanding deepens as we consider other passages in which Luke used this word, *semeron*, today, in his gospel. The word can mean either the "today" that is this particular date or the "today" of this season in life, these days, this present age. Or both at once! The angel told the shepherds, in a more literal translation of 2: 11, "For to you has been born today a savior, who is Christ the Lord." This language works, of course, as the particular day of Jesus' nativity. But it also implies more, a today that spans Jesus' life of obedience and sacrifice in which he accomplishes all that makes him the present savior and Lord. The "today" of Christ's birthday opens to the "today" of his saving ministry. Similarly, in 4: 21, after reading aloud the prophecy of Isaiah about the Messiah who would bring liberty to captives and sight to the blind, Jesus declared, "Today this Scripture has been fulfilled in your hearing." His presence as incarnate God meant its fulfillment in that very hour, and yet, as Luke tells the story, Jesus had not yet performed any liberating miracles. The "today" of that moment would be fulfilled through the coming years of mighty deeds. Also, midway through the gospel, Luke records Jesus' speaking of conducting his healing work "today and tomorrow, and the third day I finish my course" (Luke 13: 31). He means not only this calendar day but this entire phase of his life, on the way to the "tomorrow" of crucifixion and then its turn toward resurrection triumph on the third day. So *semeron* can imply both the "today" that is right now and the "today" yet to be fulfilled. Such coming fulfillment, however, is guaranteed by what is present, or occurring, this very day. In this context, his words to the thief on the cross do not have to mean Paradise on that calendar day of Good Friday. But due to the victory of his sacrifice, the entire "today" of Christ's kingdom, in all its future glory will be opened by the events of that hour to the thief and indeed to all who trust Jesus.

In fact, it is the reality of the impending furthest descent of Jesus that opens up the meaning in this poignant scene. We may imagine that the thief had a traditional Hebraic view of death as portrayed in the psalms. What if that darkest lament, Psalm 88, was on the minds and hearts of both men on the cross? The psalmist writes as a man whose "life draws near to Sheol" (vs. 3). He feels already discarded to the pit. He has become a man who is:

> Like those whom you remember no more,
> For they are cut off from your hand (vs. 5).

One of the great fears of death was being cut off not only from life in the world but from God himself, as if we get expunged even from God's thoughts. When the thief entreats Jesus to *remember* him, it is a plea to remain in existence, not to be left to utter darkness, for to be forgotten by God would mean being *cut off* from God's presence. It amazes me to consider how Jesus' reply matches the mirror-like parallel of Psalm 88: 5. The thief asks to be remembered. Jesus answers, "You will be with me." In other words, "You will not be cut off from God's hand. I will enter the experience of that utter forsakenness so that you will not."

So, the heart of this scene is that the penitent thief was united to Jesus via his faithful request. He would not be left to the isolation of separation from God. Rather, he would receive all the benefits of Jesus' journey through death and into glory.

SELECT BIBLIOGRAPHY

Alfeyev, Archbishop Hilarion. *Christ the Conqueror of Hell: The Descent into Hades from an Orthodox Perspective.* Crestwood, NY: St. Vladimir's Seminary Press, 2009.

Allender, Dan and Longman, Tremper III. *The Cry of the Soul: How Our Emotions Reveal Our Deepest Questions About God.* Carol Stream, IL: NavPress, 1999.

Aslanof, Catherine. *The Incarnate God: The Feasts of Jesus Christ and the Virgin Mary, Vols 1 & 2.* Cresco, NY: St. Vladimir's Seminary Press, 1995.

Balthasar, Hans Urs von. *Mysterium Paschale: The Mystery of Easter.* Translated by Aidan Nichols. San Francisco: Ignatius Press, 1970.

———. *The Heart of the World.* Translated by Erasmo S. Leiva. San Francisco: Ignatius Press, 1979.

———. *The Von Balthasar Reader.* Edited by Medard Kehl and Werner Loser and translated by Robert Daly and Fred Laurence. New York: Crossroad, 1982.

Bass, Justin W. *The Battle for the Keys: Revelation 1:18 and Christ's Descent into the Underworld.* Eugene, OR: Wipf and Stock Publishers, 2014.

Bates, Matthew. *The Birth of the Trinity: Jesus, God and Spirit in the New Testament and Early Christian Interpretation of the Old Testament*. Oxford: Oxford University Press, 2015.

Benedict XVI. *Jesus of Nazareth*. New York: Doubleday, 2007.

——. "Public Address, January 1, 2013." Vatican Radio. http://en.radiovaticana.va/storico/2013/01/13/pope_benedict_may_we_be_renewed_in_our_baptism/en1 655297 (accessed July 13, 2015).

——. *The Faith*. Edited by Paul Thigpen. Huntington, IN: Our Sunday Visitor, Inc., 2013.

Calvin, John. *Institutes of Christian Religion*. Edited by John T. McNeil. Translated by Ford Lewis Battles. 1559. Reprint, Philadelphia: Westminster Press, 1960.

Cantalamessa, Raniero. *Easter in the Early Church: An Anthology of Jewish and Early Christian Texts*. Collegeville, MN: The Liturgical Press, 1993.

——. *The Fire of Christ's Love: Meditations on the Cross*. Frederick, MD: The Word Among Us Press, 2013.

——. *The Holy Spirit in the Life of Jesus*. Collegeville, MN: The Liturgical Press, 1994.

——. *Life in Christ*. Collegeville, MN: The Liturgical Press, 1990.

——. *The Mystery of Easter*. Collegeville, MN: The Liturgical Press, 1993.

Catechism of the Catholic Church. New York: Doubleday, 1995.

Chrysostom, John. "Easter Sermon" Early Church Texts. http://www.earlychurchtexts.com/public/john_chrysostom easter_sermon.htm (accessed October 12, 2015).

Dawson, Gerrit. *Love Bade Me Welcome: Daily Readings with George Herbert.* Lenoir, NC: Glen Lorien Books, 1997.

Divine Liturgy According to St. John Chrysostom, 2nd ed. Translated by Russian Orthodox Greek Catholic Church of America. South Canaan, PA: St. Tikhon's Seminary Press, 1977.

Ferguson, Everett. *Baptism in the Early Church.* Grand Rapids: William B. Eerdmans Publishing Company, 2009.

Gregory of Nazianzen. "On The Baptism of Christ." 4th century. Daily Scripture Reading website. http://www.rc.net/wcc/readings/gregory-nazianzen-baptism-of-christ.htm (accessed July 13, 2015).

Grudem, Wayne. "He Did Not Descend into Hell: A Plea for Following Scripture Instead of the Apostles' Creed." *Journal of the Evangelical Theological Society* 34, no. 1 (March, 1991): 103-113.

"Gospel of Nicodemus." *The Ante-Nicene Fathers*, Vol. 1. Edited by Alexander Roberts and James Donaldson, American editor, A. Cleveland Coxe. Edinburgh: T & T Clark and Grand Rapids: William B. Eerdmans, 1993.

Hamm, Jeffery L. "*Descendit:* Delete or Declare? A Defense Against the Neo Deletionists." *Westminster Journal of Theology.* 78 (2016): 93-116.

Hummel, Bradford S. "Why at Caesarea Phillipi?" *Biblical Illustrator.* Nashville: Lifeway, Spring, 2012. 35-38.

Hyde, Daniel. *In Defense of the Descent: A Response to Contemporary Critics.* Grand Rapids: Reformation Heritage Books, 2010.

Irenaeus. "Against Heresies." *The Ante-Nicene Fathers,* Vol. 1. Edited by Alexander Roberts and James Donaldson, American editor A. Cleveland Coxe. Edinburgh: T & T Clark and Grand Rapids: William B. Eerdmans, 1993.

Kartsonis, Anna D. *Anastasis: The Making of an Image.* Princeton: Princeton University Press, 1986.

Kay, James. "He Descended into Hell." *Word and World,* vol. 31, no. 1, Winter 2011. 17-26.

Kelly, Douglas F. *Systematic Theology Volume Two: The Beauty of Christ.* Fearn: Christian Focus Publications, Inc., 2014.

Lauber, David. *Barth on the Descent into Hell: God, Atonement and the Christian Life.* Burlington, VT: Ashgate Publishing Company, 2004.

Laufer, Catherine Ella. *Hell's Destruction: An Exploration of Christ's Descent to the Dead.* Burlington, VT: Ashgate Publishing Company, 2013.

Lewis, Alan E. *Between Cross and Resurrection: A Theology of Holy Saturday.* Grand Rapids: William B. Eerdmans Publishing Company, 2001.

Lewis, C. S. "A Letter to Mary Van Deusen." Will Vaus Blogspot. http://willvausblogspot.com/2014/04/c-s-lewis-on christs-descent-into-hellhtml (accessed June 10, 2015).

Luther, Martin. "The Torgau Sermon on Christ's Descent into Hell and the Resurrection." *Sources and Contexts of the Book of Concord,* Robert Kolb & James Arne Nestingen, eds. Robert Kolb, trans. Philadelphia: Fortress Press, 2001, pp. 245-255.

MacCulloch, J.A. *The Harrowing of Hell: A Comparative Study of an Early Christian Doctrine*. Edinburgh: T&T Clark, 1930.

Macarius of Egypt. *Fifty Spiritual Homilies of Macarius the Egyptian*. Translated by A. J. Mason. London: SPCK, 1921.

Marshall, I. Howard. *1 Peter*. The IVP New Testament Commentary Series. Edited by Grant R. Osborne, D. Stuart Briscoe and Haddon Robinson. Downers Grove: InterVarsity Press, 1991.

Marshall, Taylor. "Did Christ Suffer in Hell When He Descended into Hell?" http://taylormarshall.com/2013/03/did-christ-suffer-in-hell-when-he.html (accessed March 3, 2015).

Martin, Regis. *The Suffering of Love: Christ's Descent into the Hell of Human Hopelessness*. San Francisco: Ignatius Press, 2006.

Moltmann, Jurgen. "The Presence of God's Future: The Risen Christ." *Anglican Theological Review* 89, no. 4 (Fall 2007): 577-588.

Morey, Robert A. *Death and the Afterlife*. Minneapolis: Bethany House Publishers, 1984.

Oakes, Edward T. "The Internal Logic of Holy Saturday in the Theology of Hans Urs von Balthasar." *International Journal of Systematic Theology* 9, no. 2 (April 2007): 184-199.

Ouspensky, Leonid and Lossky, V. *The Meaning of Icons*. Translated by G. E. H. Palmer and E. Kadloubovsky. Crestview, NY: St. Vladimir's Seminary Press, 1983.

Pfatteicher, Phillip H. *Journey into the Heart of God: Living the Liturgical Year*. Oxford: Oxford University Press, 2013.

Pitre, Brant. *Jesus and the Jewish Roots of the Eucharist: Unlocking the Secrets of the Last Supper*. New York: Doubleday, 2011.

Pitstick, Alyssa Lyra. *Light in Darkness: Hans Urs von Balthasar and the Catholic Doctrine of Christ's Descent into Hell*. Grand Rapids: William B. Eerdmans Publishing Company, 2007.

Pitstick, Lyra. *Christ's Descent into Hell: John Paul II, Joseph Ratzinger and Hans Urs Von Balthasar on the Theology of Holy Saturday*. Grand Rapids: William B. Eerdmans Publishing Company, 2016.

Powell, Doug. "Did Jesus 'Descend into Hell'?" http://theapologeticsgroup.com/wp-content/uploads/2012/06/Did-Jesus-Descend-Into-Hell.pdf (accessed March 3, 2015).

Ratzinger, Joseph, *Introduction to Christianity*. Translated by J.R. Foster and Michael J. Miller. San Francisco: Ignatius Press, 1968, 2004.

Reardon, Patrick Henry. *Reclaiming the Atonement: An Orthodox Theology of Redemption, Volume 1*. Chesterton, IN: Ancient Faith Publishing, 2015.

Reeves, Michael. *Rejoicing in Christ*. Downers Grove: IVP Academic, 2015.

Sanders, John. *No Other Name: Can Only Christians Be Saved?* Grand Rapids: Eerdmans Publishing Company, 1992.

Scaer, David P. "He Did Descend to Hell: In Defense of the Apostles' Creed." *Journal of the Evangelical Theological Society* 35, no. 1 (March, 1992): 91-99.

Tolkien, J.R.R. *The Letters of J.R.R. Tolkien.* Edited by Humphrey Carpenter. Boston: Houghton Mifflin Company, 1981.

———. *The Silmarillion.* Boston: Houghton Mifflin, 1977.

———. "On Fairy Stories," *Essays Presented to Charles Williams.* Edited by C. S. Lewis. Grand Rapids: William B. Eerdman's Publishing Company, 1966.

Torrance, T. F. *Theology in Reconstruction.* London: SCM Press, 1965.

Vanderlaan, Ray. "The Path to the Cross." Disc 11. *That the World May Know*, DVD. Directed by Focus on the Family. Grand Rapids: Zondervan, 2010.

_____. "Gates of Hell." http://v2.followtherabbi.com/journey/ faith-lesson/gates-of-hell (accessed April 5, 2016).

Westminster Confession of Faith: The Larger and Shorter Catechisms. The Publications Committee of the Free Presbyterian Church of Scotland, 1970.

Wright, N. T. *The Resurrection of the Son of God.* Minneapolis: Fortress Press, 2003.

_____. *Surprised by Hope: Rethinking Heaven, the Resurrection and the Mission of the Church.* New York: HarperCollins, 2008.

Yates, John. "He Descended into Hell: Creed, Article and Scripture, Part I." *Churchman*: 240-250. http://www.biblicalstudies org.uk/pdf churchman/102-03_240.pdf (accessed April 4, 2014).

ENDNOTES

Introducing the Descent

[1]In this study, regarding human beings, I consider *soul* and *spirit* as virtually synonymous in meaning and use them interchangeably.

[2]Melito of Sardis, *On the Pascha*, 102, as cited in Raniero Cantalamessa, *Easter in the Early Church* (Collegeville, MD: The Liturgical Press, 1993), 45.

[3]An old English carol captures this complexity in simple language as it hymns the victory of:
> He whose path no records tell,
> Who descended into hell,
> Who the strong man armed hath bound,
> Now in highest heaven is crowned, Alleluia!

Michael Weisse, trans. Catherine Winkworth, "Christ the Lord Is Risen Again," www.hymnary.org, April 11, 2018.

[4]Gehenna is the word translated as *hell* in the New Testament in such warning passages as Matthew 5: 22, 29, 30, 10: 28, Luke 12: 5 and Mark 9: 43. The reality of gehenna is described as the lake of fire in Revelation 19: 20 and 20: 10. See Appendix 1 for a more detailed explanation of these Biblical terms translated often as "hell."

[5]"For, since he 'died for our sins and rose for our justification,' as the apostle says, (Rom. 4: 25), a certain passage from death to life has been consecrated in the passion and resurrection of the Lord." Augustine, "Letter 55, To Januarius," AD 400, as quoted in Raniero

Cantalamessa, *Easter in the Early Church* (Collegeville, MN: The Liturgical Press, 1993), 109. Also, "For by suffering the Lord made the passage from death to life and opened a way for us who believe in his resurrection by which we too might pass from death to life." Augustine "Exposition of Psalm 120," as quoted in Cantalamessa, *Easter in the Early Church*, 109.

Chapter 1   Biblical and Theological Sources

[6]See Appendix 1 for a more detailed explanation of these Biblical terms.

[7]The Roman Catholic Catechism clearly summarizes this in words that all apostolic traditions can accept:

> In his plan of salvation, God ordained that his Son should not only "die for our sins" but should also "taste death," experience the condition of death, the separation of his soul from his body, between the time he expired on the cross and the time he was raised from the dead. . . .

> The frequent New Testament affirmations that Jesus was "raised from the dead" presuppose that the crucified one sojourned in the realm of the dead prior to his resurrection. This was the first meaning given in the apostolic preaching to Christ's descent into hell: that Jesus, like all men, experienced death and in his soul joined the others in the realm of the dead. (*Catechism of the Roman Catholic Church*, New York: Doubleday, 1995, 624, 632.)

[8]The abyss (*abussos*) here means at the least to the place of the dead, metaphorically in the deeps under the earth or sea. Paul may or may not mean the place where demonic beings dwell (Rev. 11: 7) or to which they are banished (Luke 8: 31, Rev. 20: 3). See *Dictionary of Biblical Imagery* (Downers Grove: IVP: 1998, 200-201), Justin Bass, *The Battle for the Keys* (Eugene: Wipf and Stock, 2014), 74-77, and *Theological Dictionary of the New Testament*, vol.

1, Gerhard Kittel, ed., Geoffrey Bromiley, trans. (Grand Rapids: William B. Eerdmans, 1964), 9-10.

[9]The ESV has actually changed its original translation of "the lower parts of the earth" to "the lower regions, the earth," with the ESV Study Bible (Crossway). Justin Bass notes that the more ancient reading is of the "netherworld," with the "earth" gaining traction more recently. He cites many sources for both views in *Battle for the Keys*, 77-78. W.H. Griffith Thomas notes simply, "There are two views of this passage, some interpreting it of our Lord's descent to earth in the Incarnation, and others a descent into the unseen world." *Principles of Theology* (London: Vine Books, 1930), 67.

[10]Phillip Schaff, *The Creeds of Christendom with a History and Critical Notes, vol 2; The History of the Creeds* (New York: Harper and Row, 1889), 45.

[11]Matthew Bates' seminal work, *The Birth of the Trinity* (Oxford: Oxford University Press, 2015) uncovers the exegetical practice of the ancient church, including the New Testament writers. As they read the Hebrew Scriptures in the light of Christ, the first Christians overheard conversations between the divine persons. The Old Testament came alive as a *theodrama*, in which the divine characters took the stage in the words of prophets speaking ahead of the redemption to be accomplished in the incarnate work of the Son of God. Bates skillfully opens up new depths of meaning in Jesus' quotations of Psalm 22, 110, 166 and others. So, in regard to our topic, he draws out how Psalm 22 shows that "the Son is truly *abandoned unto death*, and cries out 'Why?' in the face of felt futility, but even while hurling forth these words of despair in his moment of deepest darkness, he knows the playwright—the Spirit—and he is aware of the [triumphant] conclusion of the script" (130).

[12]*The Odes of Solomon* imagine Jesus saying, "Death ejected me and many with me. I have been vinegar and bitterness to it" (Ode 42). John Chrysostom would graphically preach, "That Body, which [Death] could not digest, he received; and therefore had to cast forth that which he had within him. Yea, he travailed in pain, whilst

He held him, and was straitened until he vomited him up" (*Homilies on First Corinthians*, 24: 7).

[13]*Divine Liturgy According to St. John Chrysostom*, 2nd ed., Russian Orthodox Greek Catholic Church of America, trans, (South Canaan, PA: St. Tikhon's Seminary Press, 1977), 153.

[14]For an excellent summary of the discussion on this passage, see I. Howard Marshall, *1 Peter*, ed. Grant R. Osborne, D. Stuart Briscoe and Haddon Robinson (Downer's Grove: InterVarsity Press, 1991), 117-139.

[15]Calvin scoffed at the notion of a harrowing: "But this story, although it is repeated by great authors ... still is nothing but a story. It is childish to enclose the souls of the dead in a prison. What need, then, for Christ's soul to go down to release them?" John Calvin, *Institutes of the Christian Religion*, ed., John T. McNeil, trans., Ford Lewis Battles (1559, repr., Philadelphia: Westminster Press, 1960), 2.16.9.

[16]John Calvin, *Institutes of the Christian Religion*, ed., John T. McNeil, trans., Ford Lewis Battles (1559, repr., Philadelphia: Westminster Press, 1960), 2.16.10, 11.

[17]"Because he is an infinite person, his suffering of hell for these three hours of outer darkness have been more than sufficient to exhaust all the fires and dark horrors of the infernal realm, as certainly as though a finite person had been consigned to its dread conditions for an endless eternity." Douglas Kelly, *Systematic Theology, Vol. 2: The Beauty of Christ* (Fearn, Scotland: Christian Focus, 2014), 381.

[18]Thomas Torrance, *Theology in Reconstruction*, (London: SCM Press, 1965), 124.

[19]*Westminster Confession of Faith: The Larger and Shorter Catechisms*, (The Publications Committee of the Free Presbyterian Church of Scotland, 1970), 152-153.

[20]Hans Urs Von Balthasar, *The Von Balthasar Reader*, Medard Kehl and Werner Loser, eds. and Robert Daly and Fred Laurence, trans., (New York: Crossroad, 1982), 153.

[21]Hans Urs Von Balthasar, *Mysterium Paschale: The Mystery of Easter*, trans. Aidan Nichols (San Francisco: Ignatius Press, 1990), 161.

[22]Alyssa Lyra Pitstick is the most notable opponent. See her *Light in Darkness* and *Christ's Descent into Hell* for a full critique.

[23]For example, see *The Suffering of Love* by Regis Martin, *Between Cross and Resurrection* by Alan Lewis, *Barth on the Descent into Hell* (which has a surprising amount on Balthasar!) by David Lauber, and *Hell's Destruction* by Catherine Laufer.

[24]Benedict XVI, *The Faith*, ed., Paul Thigpen (Huntington, IN: Our Sunday Visitor, Inc., 2013), 84-85.

[25]Catherine Ella Laufer, *Hell's Destruction: An Exploration of Christ's Descent to the Dead* (Burlington: Ashgate Publishing Company, 2013), 190, italics mine. I am heartily grateful for Laufer's work. In the many cases where I've read her primary sources, I've found Laufer's explanations to be accurate. Moreover, to date, she is the only theologian to have systematically compared the sources of belief about the descent through the centuries. Her rigorous work in synthesizing the often competing views has given future theologians a solid platform upon which to build, fulfilling the expressed hope of her work (197). The constraints of my own confessional tradition do not allow me to share, except in the heart's desire, her final conclusion of a near universal salvation. Yet Laufer carefully separates her personal conclusion from her account and summary of the doctrine's interpretations to date.

[26]Christina Rossetti, "The Love of Christ Which Passeth Knowledge," *The Complete Works of Christina Rossetti*, vol 1, (Baton Rouge: Louisiana State University Press, 1979), 66.

Chapter 2 Leaping Down into Our Life

[27]Gregory the Great (d. 604), Homily 29, *Forty Gospel Homilies*, trans. Dom David Hurst (Kalamazoo: Cistercian Publications, 1990), 234.

[28]William G. Storey, *Prayers of Christian Consolation* (Chicago: Loyola Press, 2010), 186.

[29]See Raniero Cantalamessa, *The Mystery of Easter* (Collegeville, MN: The Liturgical Press, 1993), 14-18. And Phillip Pffatteicher *Journey into the Heart of God: Living the Liturgical Year* (Oxford: Oxford University Press, 2013), 215-216.

[30]Through the centuries, Christ's church has come to call the celebration of this transit the Triduum, the three holy days across which the one, unified event of our redemption occurred. See Pfatteicher, *Journey into the Heart of God*, "the Holy Triduum [is] the unified celebration (Good Friday, Holy Saturday, Easter Day) of the death, the rest in the tomb and resurrection of Christ as one event," 13. Also 193 and 226.

[31]See, for example, Irenaeus, *Against Heresies, 5. Pref.*, Athanasius, *Against the Arians*, 4.7, and Gregory Nazianzen, *Theological Oration* 1.5.

[32]Translation from the traditional *Book of Common Prayer*, Church of England, 1662.

[33]Benedict XVI, Public Address, January 1, 2013, Vatican Radio, http://en.radiovaticana.va/storico/2013/01/13/pope_benedict_may_we_be_renewed_in_our_baptism/en1-655297 (accessed July 13, 2015).

[34]Ray Vanderlaan, "Gates of Hell," That the World Might Know, http://v2.followtherabbi.com/journey/faith-lesson/gates-of-hell (accessed April 5, 2016).

[35]Bradford S. Hummel, "Why at Caesarea Phillipi?" *Biblical Illustrator.* Nashville: Lifeway, Spring, 2012. 35-38.

[36]Everett Ferguson, *Baptism in the Early Church* (Grand Rapids: William B. Eerdmans Publishing Company, 2009), 120.

[37]Benedict XVI, *Jesus of Nazareth: The Infancy Narratives,* (New York: Image Publishing, 2012), 20.

[38]Gregory of Nazianzen, "On The Baptism of Christ," 4th century, Daily Scripture Reading website, http://www.rc.net/wcc/readings/gregory-nazianzen-baptism-of-christ.htm (accessed July 13, 2015).

Chapter 3   Down to the Captives

[39]While this story does not appear in the earliest manuscripts of the fourth gospel, it yet remains part of the text the church recognized as canonical and I am treating it as such.

[40]The Greek word used here, *esplanchnisthe,* means to be deeply moved in the center of one's being. Graphically, it implies being stirred in one's guts.

[41]C.S. Lewis, *Miracles,* (New York: MacMillan and Sons, 1947), chp 14.

[42]Ibid.

Chapter 4   Straining the Eternal Bonds

[43]Cyrillonas, *First Homily on the Pascha,* as quoted in Cantalamessa, *Easter in the Early Church,* 85-86.

[44]Especially if one compares Mark (or Matt. 26: 38) with the Septuagint, the Greek Old Testament of the time.

[45]Ray Vanderlaan, "The Path to the Cross," Disc 11, *That the World May Know*, DVD, directed by Focus on the Family (Grand Rapids: Zondervan, 2010).

[46]Cantalamessa, *The Mystery of Easter*, 23.

[47]Compare how Balthasar imagines Jesus describing his experience in *The Heart of the World* (San Francisco: Ignatius Press, 1979), 175:

> ... with each throb my Heart became more desolate, strength poured out from me in streams and there remained only faintness, death's fatigue, infinite failure, and at last I neared that mysterious and final spot on the very edge of being, and then—the fall into the void, the capsizing into the bottomless abyss, the vertigo, the finale, the un-becoming: that colossal death which only I have died. Through my death this has been spared you, and no one will ever experience what it really means to die: This was my victory.

[48]Francis Spufford, *Unapologetic: Why, Despite Everything, Christianity Can Still Make Surprising Emotional Sense* (New York: Harper One, 2013), 141.

[49]For example, if I were in an extreme situation, and could only whisper, "Amazing grace," how would you interpret what I meant? Surely you would finish the verse: "How sweet the sound, that saved a wretch like me. I once was lost but now am found. . . ." The full verse would lend explanation as to why the two words came from my lips.

[50]Contra Alan Lewis and Jurgen Moltman. Affirmed with Torrance, Balthasar and Barth.

[51]Douglas F. Kelly, *Systematic Theology Volume Two: The Beauty of Christ* (Fearn: Christian Focus Publications, Inc., 2014), 384.

[52]Raniero Cantalamessa, *The Fire of Christ's Love: Meditations on the Cross* (Frederick, MD: The Word Among Us Press, 2013), 42.

[53]Kelly, *Systematic Theology*, 402.

[54]e.g., Thomas Torrance, *Theology in Reconstruction*, 125.

[55]Ibid. "'Father'—that had been the answer of his whole life on earth, the answer of the obedient Son, for through the whole course of his obedience from birth to death he bent our human nature back into a perfectly filial relation of faith and truth toward the Father. 'Not my will, but thine be done.'"

[56]George Herbert, "Prayer Before Sermon," *The Complete English Poems*, John Tobin, ed. (New York: Penguin Books, 1991), 261.

Chapter 5 Dead Stop Saturday

[57]Cf. " . . . we have been sanctified through the offering of the body of Jesus *once for all* . . . But when Christ had offered for all time *a single sacrifice for sins*, he sat down at the right hand of God" (Heb. 10: 10, 12).

[58]Calvin, *Institutes*, 2.16.5.

[59]In that culture's reckoning of time, Sunday officially began after sunset on Saturday (twenty-seven hours after Jesus' death at 3 p.m. Friday), though the dawn of Sunday was considered to be around 6 a.m. (thirty-nine hours after his death), near to when the women first encountered the risen Lord. Hence, as we count time from our perspective in the realm of this world, Jesus' resurrection occurred between twenty-seven and thirty-nine hours after his death. Also in that culture, parts of days were counted as full days, so he could be considered dead for three days if were dead anytime Friday, Saturday and Sunday.

[60]Laufer, *Hell's Destruction*, 199.

[61]We note the lovely words of an ancient homily quoted in the Roman Catholic Catechism, par. 635: "Today a great silence reigns

on earth, a great silence and a great stillness. A great silence because the King is asleep. The earth trembled and is still because God has fallen asleep in the flesh . . ."

[62]The Orthodox emphasis on Jesus' triumph in Sheol rests on the historic understanding of the hypostatic union. Jesus separated from his body yet remained fully human and fully divine in soul. Indeed, on this all Nicene/Constantinopolitan Christians agree. From here, the Orthodox go on to ask how Death could ever capture or hold the one united to Life itself. Of course, this is ultimately true, as we shall explore in the next chapter. The Orthodox conclusion thereby disallows any passivity on the part of Christ in Sheol. But the mystery of the kenosis of the Son of God did not end at his death. It was just as impossible that the divine Son could take up flesh and that the fully divine/fully human Jesus could die physically while joined forever to the everlasting life of the Son of God. But in both cases he did. So too, he could, for a season, engage the passivity of human death in the realm of the dead.

[63]It is, of course, beyond the scope of this project to analyze all of Balthasar's theology, or even to comment on all his thought regarding Jesus' descent to hell. One need not agree with every aspect of Balthasar's theology (such as his nuanced belief in purgatory or his pushing the boundaries toward universalism) in order to draw from his insights into Holy Saturday.

[64]Balthasar, *Mysterium Paschale*, 161. Balthasar resists the word "descends" for Jesus' entrance into Sheol because he considers it too active for the dead Christ, speaking instead of his "going to the dead," 150. See also Lauber, *Barth on the Descent*, 66-67.

[65]Ibid. 137-8. "For the redeeming act consists in a wholly unique bearing of the total sin of the world by the Father's wholly unique Son . . . in that absolutely unique man who is unique because he is God, and who . . . can communicate a share in his Cross to his fellow human beings, with whom he is more profoundly solitary than any man can ever be with any other man, and can do that in death itself, where each man is absolutely alone."

[66]Ibid., 51-52.

[67]Ibid., 173.

[68]Lauber, *Barth on the Descent*, 72.

[69]*Westminster Confession.*

[70]Balthasar, *Mysterium Paschale*, 150.

[71]Lauber, *Barth on the Descent into Hell*, 69-70, 85.

[72]Perhaps in remaining under the power of death, Jesus merely slept. Or maybe he waited in the numbness of Sheol without despair. Perhaps. In that case, the hiatus of Holy Saturday yet forces us to contemplate the meaning of the cross after the dismaying intensity of his suffering, but before the victorious release of his rising. This remains the day of waiting without hope. But I believe a strong case has been made that this is also the way Jesus himself waited. If I am wrong, then at the least, we have yet taken the meaning of Good Friday further into this Sabbath during which a new creation gestated.

[73]Joseph Ratzinger, *Introduction to Christianity*, trans., J. R. Foster and Michael J. Miller (San Francisco: Ignatius Press, 1968), 294. "This saying of Nietzsche's belongs linguistically to the tradition of Christian Passiontide piety; it expresses the content of Holy Saturday, 'descended into hell.'"

Chapter 6 Sunday Before Sunrise

[74]Pfatteicher, *Journey Into the Heart of God*, 232. See also Benedict XVI, *The Faith*, 80.

[75]In Hebrew, Greek and Latin, as well as English, "arise" carries the meaning of both waking up and getting up. The root of the Hebrew word used, *quts*, can mean both awake and arise. In Greek, *egeiro*

can mean both arising and waking, getting up and coming awake from sleep. The word *anistemi* refers more to getting up physically, but, of course, that can be from a bed where one has slept. In Latin, *resurgo*, the root of *resurrexi*, means both get up and rise up, from either sleep or lying down.

[76] A. Lewis, *Between Cross and Resurrection*, 224.

[77] Cantalamessa, *Life in Christ*, 75.

[78] For instance, regarding 3: 16, the word Peter used for "spirits" was everywhere else associated with heavenly beings, and even if Peter means the dead, there is question whether it is *all* the dead or just the ones literally from Noah's time. Regarding 4: 6, a conceptual "now" is inserted for interpretation, insisting that Peter meant that the gospel had been preached earlier to those dead at the time of his writing. These alternate readings to the traditional message to the dead can get no more purchase than the historic interpretation, but they do serve to call that tradition into question, *as regards these texts*. However, as we have seen, the overall context of Scripture and the trajectory of Jesus-history supports some addressing of the question of when and how the gospel that is the life, death and resurrection of Jesus was made known to the spirits of those who died awaiting a Redeemer.

[79] Enoch who was taken up by God (Gen. 5: 24) and Elijah who was "taken up by a whirlwind into heaven" (2 Kings 2: 11) are the notable exceptions. Their apparent skipping over of a sojourn in Sheol makes awkward any neat, definitive statements we might make about a state in which we have so little knowledge.

[80] The intermediate destiny after death of those outside of Christ is little addressed in Scripture (it's not clear if Jesus' parable in Luke 16 of Lazarus and the rich man is meant to give cosmological information). Jesus chillingly speaks, however, of the future resurrection this way, " . . . an hour is coming when all who are in the tombs will hear his voice and come out, those who have done good to the resurrection of life, and those who have done evil to the

resurrection of judgment" (John 5: 28-9). *The Westminster Catechism* confidently, perhaps overconfidently, imports this future judgment into the intermediate state of those outside Christ, "On the other hand, when the wicked die, their souls are thrown into hell. There they remain tormented in complete darkness, while their bodies are kept in the grave as in a prison, until the resurrection and judgment of that great day" (Answer 86). This assertion seems to be based on the fate of fallen angels as described in 2 Peter 2: 4 and Jude 6 more than on a particular teaching about the intermediate state of humans.

[81]Of course it can be argued that departing from this realm, one's spirit leaves time the way we reckon it, and hence one could step right into the resurrected body even though that general resurrection has not yet occurred in the space/time realm of this earth. That would be fine with me, but any definitive assertion seems speaking beyond what we are able. For a stimulating look at the importance of embodied life *after* life after death, see N. T. Wright, *Surprised by Hope: Rethinking Heaven, the Resurrection and the Mission of the Church* (New York: HarperCollins, 2008).

[82]Chrysostom, *Divine Liturgy*, 181.

[83]Patrick Henry Reardon, *Reclaiming the Atonement: An Orthodox Theology of Redemption, Vol. 1* (Chesterton, IN: Ancient Faith Publishing, 2015). Reardon's chapter on Christ and Adam provided great focus for this and the following section.

[84]Calvin, *Institutes*, 2.16.5.

[85]Michael Reeves, *Christ Our Life* (Crownhill, Milton Keynes: Paternoster, 2014), 41.

[86]Irenaeus, "Against Heresies," *The Ante-Nicene Fathers*, Vol. 1, eds., Alexander Roberts and James Donaldson, American ed., A. Cleveland Coxe (Edinburgh: T & T Clark and Grand Rapids: William B. Eerdmans, 1993), 3.18.1.

[87]Ibid., 3.18.7.

[88]Ibid., 5.14.3.

[89]Ibid., 3.19.4 and 3.23.

[90]Ibid., 2.22.4.

[91]Catechism of the Catholic Church, answer 635, attributed to an anonymous 4th century sermon.

[92]Leonid Ouspensky and Vladimir Lossky, *The Meaning of Icons*, trans. G. E. H. Palmer and E. Kadloubovsky (Crestview, NY: St. Vladimir's Seminary Press, 1983), 188.

[93]Emphatically, we do not, as does for example Dominic Crossan, declare that the *meaning* of the resurrection is what matters more than the *mode* of Jesus' rising. The actuality of Jesus rising in the body that was crucified in the real world where we live is bedrock to our faith. So, for me, is the actuality of the particular Adam. It is precisely when we grasp, through Scripture and historic confessions, these anchor points, that we can then handle what is imaginative safely, finding the spiritual meaning in prayers, narratives, poems and images that reach beyond the known. Our ability to distinguish what is literal (but laden with symbolic import) from what is purely symbolic makes possible the theological use of such imaginative work. See *The Resurrection of Jesus: John Dominic Crossan and N.T. Wright in Dialogue*, ed. Robert Stewart (Minneapolis: Fortress Press, 2006), 16-47.

[94]"The Gospel of Nicodemus," *The Ante-Nicene Fathers*, Vol. 1, edited by Alexander Roberts and James Donaldson, American editor, A. Cleveland Coxe (Edinburgh: T & T Clark and Grand Rapids: William B. Eerdmans, 1993), Latin 2nd version, chapter 9.

Chapter 7   Descending to the World's Hell

[95]Gregory the Great, uncited homily, as quoted in Balthasar, *Mysterium Paschale*, 175.

[96]Macarius of Egypt, *Fifty Spiritual Homilies of Macarius the Egyptian,* trans., A. J. Mason (London: SPCK, 1921), Homily 11, sections 11-12.

[97]Ibid.

[98]It would be interesting to study Macarius in more detail to see if elsewhere he articulates that even our desire to seek God is a gift from him. In the homily considered here, Macarius seems unperturbed by holding together Jesus' quickening of dead people with the idea that those spiritually dead people were saved because they were "seeking God."

[99]Ratzinger, *Introduction to Christianity,* 298.

[100]Ibid., 300.

[101]Ibid., 301.

[102]Catherine Aslanof, *The Incarnate God: The Feasts of Jesus Christ and the Virgin Mary, Vol 2.* (Cresco, NY: St. Vladimir's Seminary Press, 1995), 141.

[103]Dan Allender and Tremper Longman deftly related Jesus' descent into hell to the spiritual formation of our suffering. See *The Cry of the Soul: How our Emotions Reveal Our Deepest Questions About God,* (Carol Stream, IL: NavPress, 1999), 156-158.

[104]Francis Spufford, *Unapologetic,* 146.

[105]Cantalamessa, *Life in Christ,* 70-71.

[106]Matthew Bridges, "Crown Him with Many Crowns," Hymnary, http://www.hymnary.org/text/crown_him_with_many_crowns (accessed October 24, 2015).

[107]This is hardly an isolated text. See also all the parables in Matthew 25 and the parable of Lazarus and the rich man recorded in Luke 16: 19-25, as well as Jesus' constant warnings to repent, beginning

with Mark 1: 1.

[108]C. S. Lewis, "A Letter to Mary Van Deusen," January 31, 1952, The Lamp Post, http://willvaus.blogspot.com/2014/04/c-s-lewis-on-christs-descent-into-hell.html (accessed June 10, 2015).

[109]For more on the wider hope, see John Sanders, *No Other Name*, chapters 4-6 and Catherine Ella Laufer, *Hell's Destruction*, chapters 5-8.

[110]See Laufer, *Hell's Destruction*, pp. 137-141 for an excellent summary of such views through the history of theology.

[111]Gerrit Dawson, *Love Bade Me Welcome: Daily Readings with George Herbert*, (Lenoir, NC: Glen Lorien Books, 1997), 89.

[112]Benedict XVI, *The Faith*, 86-87.

[113]William Milligan, *The Ascension of Our Lord* (London: Macmillan & Co., 1894), 188.

[114]J.R.R. Tolkien, "Letter 89," in *The Letters of J.R.R. Tolkien*, ed. Humphrey Carpenter, (Boston: Houghton Milton, 1981), 100.

[115]J.R.R. Tolkien, "On Fairy Stories," *Essays Presented to Charles Williams*, ed. C.S. Lewis (Grand Rapids: William B. Eerdmans Publishing Company, 1966), 81-84.

[116]John Chrysostom, "Easter Sermon," Early Church Texts, http://www.earlychurchtexts.com/public/john_chrysostom_easter_sermon.htm (accessed October 12, 2015).

Appendix 1   Clarifying the Terms

[117]Contra Kenneth Hagin and Kenneth Copeland, https://www.youtube.com/watch?v=7dwbNvBq7eQ. Contra Joyce Meyer, https://www.youtube.com/watch?v=sL08t3kUEjw.

[118]Lauber, p. 67 describes this insight of Balthasar who "insists that the hell of the New Testament is Christologically determined. It is brought into existence only as a result of Jesus' experience in death."

[119]Robert A. Morey, *Death and the Afterlife* (Minneapolis: Bethany House Publishers, 1984), 78-79.

[120]We note the wealth of understanding in Martha's astute reply to Jesus about her deceased brother, "I know that he will rise again in the resurrection on the last day" (John 11: 24).

[121]The question has been highly debated as to whether Jesus meant to give information about Hades in this parable or whether he used popular imagery to make the deeper point that choices for or against love and mercy in this life have consequences in the next.

Appendix 2   The Thief on the Cross

[122]E.g., "To be reconciled to Christ is to be in paradise immediately." *The Orthodox Study Bible* (Nashville: Thomas Nelson, 2008), 1413.

[123]This possible interpretation gains plausibility when we consider other passages where "today" is added to a proclamation to intensify its urgency (cf. Deut. 7: 13, 8: 3, 9: 3, and Acts 26: 22).

[124]See Laufer, *Hell's Destruction*, 190-197.

INDEX OF BIBLICAL
REFERENCES

INDEX OF SUBJECTS AND AUTHORS

ACKNOWLEDGMENTS

count it a deep joy to pastor a congregation permeated with a culture of quest for Christ. The First Presbyterians in Baton Rouge love to worship the Triune God, to study the Scriptures and to serve Jesus by caring for his little ones. Our slogan is not an aspiration but a description of our life together, pressing "Deeper in Christ, Further into the World."

Even so, I'm amazed they would so heartily spend a season of Lent daily reading of the events of Jesus' ever deepening descent to save us and daily praying psalms from within the life of Jesus. They studied as individuals, in small groups and in Sunday worship. We all got changed. Through our work together arose this book's perspective on Jesus' descent into hell. That they gave me extra time to write up the results of this research creates further gratitude. I love to be their pastor.

Some particular thanks are due. To the pilot group that helped shape the study: Kyle Beall, Jaime Carnaggio, Bonnie Ferrell, Katie Forsthoff, Tim Hatcher, Lisa Head, Suzanne Kennon, Hank Mills, Elizabeth Parker and Joe Willis. You guys were amazing! Thanks Jesse Gellrich for sharing your knowledge of Latin and Medieval literature. Thanks to Katie Robinson and Sally McConnell for joining the publication team, it's always a joy to do projects with you. To my assistant, Jaci Gaspard, you always fill in the gaps. To my friend and research assistant, Lisa Head, I never could have done this without your hours of painstaking work.

Finally, to Rhonda, as Van Morrison sings, "Oh my dear, oh my dear sweet love, it's a long, long journey. A long, long journey home." Every step of that path I get to walk alongside you I count as precious.

Gerrit Dawson
Fairlight Tower
Brevard, North Carolina
Midsummer Day 2018